# Will You Still L In The Morning

A farce

Brian Clemens
and
Dennis Spooner

Samuel French - London
New York - Toronto - Hollywood

## CHARACTERS

**Jeremy Winthrop**
**Celia Winthrop**
**Sara Ward**
**Humphrey Jessel**
**Syd Clancy***
**Thelma Jessel**
**Peregrine Ward**
Plus 1 Male Voice (off-stage)

The action of the play takes place in the main interior of the Winthrops' country cottage.

### ACT I
A Saturday afternoon

### ACT II
Evening, the same day

*Syd Clancy may be played by a woman but references to Mrs Clancy and "the missis" will need to be changed.

# ACT I

*The main interior of the Winthrops' country cottage. Late afternoon on a Saturday*

*It is olde-worlde and elegant enough. L is the front door. Upstage and extreme R and facing us are french doors leading to the garden and the country beyond. A short flight of stairs leads up to a landing. Off this landing, and directly facing us are doors leading to two bedrooms—one R the other L. In the space between is a door to the bathroom*

*On the lower floor there is, extreme R and downstage, a door off to the kitchen. Nearby, a cellar door. (Note: If this cellar door can be partially screened or obstructed by some architectural or furnishing feature, that would be beneficial for subsequent staging)*

*There is a dining table, chairs, a sideboard, a large, deep sofa, a couple of easy chairs, together with other normal everyday furnishings*

*When the* CURTAIN *rises, the house is empty—the french doors and any windows are closed and locked. Outside it is a pleasant, balmy summer day*

*A pause—then we hear a taxi drive up—stop—a pause—then, as we hear the taxi drive away again, a key goes into the lock*

*The front door opens and Jeremy Winthrop enters carrying Celia Winthrop across the threshold. Jeremy is a diffident, albeit attractive, young man of about thirty. Celia is an attractive young woman of about twenty-five. She apparently has more "steel" in her than Jeremy—but, come the crunch, can become just as panicked. They are newly-weds and very much in love. Jeremy, carrying Celia, gets to the foot of the stairs*

**Celia** No, Jeremy, the threshold ends here.
**Jeremy** But, darling . . .
**Celia** Jeremy, not *now* . . .
**Jeremy** You've been saying that for a week.
**Celia** Put me down. Please, darling.

*He does—then tries to kiss her—she evades him*

Jeremy, our cases.

*He regards her*

You've left them outside.

*He regards her*

It might rain, Jeremy.

**Jeremy** Oh, very well ... But you stay right where you are ...

*Jeremy crosses to the front door, brings in two cases, crosses to quickly open a side cupboard, puts them away*

**Celia** But we haven't unpacked them yet!

**Jeremy** Nothing I need in there, except pyjamas ... and I won't be needing them ... (*He moves in on her again*)

**Celia** You forgot to replace the key.

*As he embraces her ...*

You know if Mrs Clancy comes here and there's no key, she'll turn right round and go home.

**Jeremy** Let her.

**Celia** But then that will mean I'll have to do all the cleaning ... and then I'll be too tired and have no time to do *anything else*.

**Jeremy** (*hesitating*) Good point! (*He hurries over to open the front door, replaces the key, closes the door and returns—predatory—towards Celia*)

**Celia** Jeremy, you're so impetuous.

**Jeremy** Impetuous!? We've been married a week, and I still haven't.

**Celia** That hasn't exactly been my fault, has it! It was *supposed* to be a *honeymoon* hotel!

**Jeremy** We both went through the brochure together. And you must admit, the hotel looked very nice.

**Celia** I'm sure it will be. When they finish building it ...

**Jeremy** And move it a bit nearer the sea. God, it *was* awful, wasn't it darling?

**Celia** It reminded me of Colditz, and I don't think I shall ever forget the food.

**Jeremy** Oh, come on, that wasn't so bad.

**Celia** That thing they served us on the first day?! Staring at me ... *all* its eyes—and so many legs!

**Jeremy** Tentacles. Squid have tentacles.

**Celia** Mine had *legs*. I'm sure it was a centipede.

**Jeremy** Rest of the food wasn't so bad though. I mean, it wasn't exactly *uneatable*.

*She gives him a look*

Only on Wednesday.

*She gives him a look*

Oh, all right ... *and* Friday. Lucky enough I had the wit to cancel our booking.

*She gives him a look*

All right, I admit it was *your* idea—but *I* had to face up to that big, brutish Spaniard ... I'm *sure* he used to be a bull-fighter—the way he held his pen.

**Celia** (*introspectively*) I'll never forget it. Never.

**Jeremy** Anyway, here we are, back in our own little home a week earlier than expected. You can't possibly be shy here.
**Celia** I wasn't shy! But I do object when I whisper something in your ear and the man in the next room replies.
**Jeremy** Yes, the walls were a bit thin. Oh, but darling, we still have a whole week of honeymoon left . . . and no-one knows we're back . . .
**Celia** Exactly. So there's no need to rush, is there?
**Jeremy** Rush? Who's rushing?
**Celia** You are. Like a . . . a bull in a china shop.
**Jeremy** You don't look much like a china shop to me, darling.
**Celia** I *feel* like a china shop. I feel . . . fragile. I haven't fully recovered from last night yet.
**Jeremy** You shouldn't have moved—I kept telling you that spiders, no matter how gigantic they are, rarely attack unless provoked.
**Celia** You kept telling me from the top of the wardrobe.
**Jeremy** Well, it was your scream—it panicked me. Anway, I thought you were awfully brave, darling . . . taking my slipper to it . . . and I *was* just getting down from the wardrobe to help . . . I mean, if it hadn't collapsed under me . . . !
**Celia** I still shudder to think about it.
**Jeremy** (*embracing her*) It's all over—behind us now. We're home and what do newly-weds do in the privacy of their own home?
**Celia** They sit down.

*She does. He moves towards her*

Jeremy—darling—I understand your frustration. But . . .

*He leaps on her—and kisses her—she pulls free*

But I am not going to start my honeymoon on a *sofa*!
**Jeremy** Then come to bed.
**Celia** I intend to.
**Jeremy** Ah!
**Celia** After we have had a civilized *English* meal . . .
**Jeremy** (*interjecting*) I'm prepared to risk it on an empty stomach.
**Celia** But not on *my* empty stomach.

*He advances on her again—but she abruptly gets up and leaves him embracing the sofa!*

Later, darling—later.

*Celia exits into the kitchen. Jeremy haplessly follows her*

*A pause—then we hear a taxi drive up and stop*

*A slight pause, then we hear a key turn in the lock, the door opens and Sara Ward enters. She is an attractive woman of about thirty-five to forty. A woman who for years has denied her sexuality and assumed an attitude of "properness"—but she is on the brink of breaking out! Nevertheless, as she fully enters the area, there is an air of trepidation about her. During this, we hear the taxi drive away again. As it does so, panic overcomes Sara, she starts to change her mind, and turns to run out again, but is confronted by ...*

*Humphrey Jessel, a handsome, extrovert man—about forty-five—charming, the kind who has great experience and a "way with women". He carries two small overnight cases, a bottle of champagne, a box of chocolates and a package*

**Humphrey** Hey, where do you think you're going?

**Sara** Humphrey, I'm sorry, but I don't think I can go through with it.

**Humphrey** Nonsense.

**Sara** I'm frightened.

**Humphrey** Of course you are. And I understand.

**Sara** You do?

**Humphrey** I do. And that's why Humphrey is here—to calm you. (*He kisses her*)

**Sara** Humphrey, you are not calming me.

*He kisses her again*

I didn't like the way that taxi driver looked at us. As though he knew we were not married ...

**Humphrey** But we are.

**Sara** But not to each other. He gave me a very searching look. I'm sure he knew.

**Humphrey** Perhaps I gave the game away when I kissed you.

**Sara** *Peregrine* kisses me sometimes.

**Humphrey** Like this?

*He kisses her again. Then she pushes him away—looking quite "fluttery"*

**Sara** The key.

**Humphrey** Eh?

**Sara** The key. (*She flourishes it*) We promised Jeremy Winthrop we'd replace the key—just in case his cleaning lady dropped by.

**Humphrey** Winthrop is on honeymoon until next weekend—why *would* his cleaning lady drop by?

**Sara** I don't know, but she might. And it was the only thing Winthrop was adamant about, "Use the place as your own, but please replace the key."

**Humphrey** Very well.

*He moves to briefly exit out of the front door—then reappears and closes the front door behind him*

Well. Alone at last.

**Sara** This will be the first time I've ever been unfaithful to Peregrine.

**Humphrey** That's encouraging.

*She reacts*

You've accepted you *are* going to be unfaithful. Sara ...

**Sara** And what about Thelma?

**Humphrey** (*stopping his advance*) Thelma! What about Thelma!?
**Sara** She's your wife.
**Humphrey** Oh ... hang, Thelma!
**Sara** Humphrey, please don't talk like that—you know perfectly well she's my very best friend. What if she found out?
**Humphrey** Darling, she isn't going to find out. Nor is Peregrine.
**Sara** But what if they did?
**Humphrey** Look—Thelma is in Bristol visiting her mother—and thinks *I* am in Munich on business. Peregrine *is* on business in Paris—and thinks *you* are in Exeter ... It's that simple.
**Sara** Humphrey——
**Humphrey** (*interjecting*) Don't you think we should unpack ...? Then a quiet drink ... a chat ...? The last thing I want to do is rush you ... but ... the sooner we *really* get ... used to each other?
**Sara** (*after hesitating*) Very well.

*They go up the stairs—then Humphrey hesitates*

**Humphrey** Which room's it to be?
**Sara** We ... ll. *Peregrine* always votes Conservative.
**Humphrey** Right. Or rather—*left!*

*Humphrey leads the way and they exit into the left-hand bedroom*

*Almost immediately, Celia and Jeremy enter from the kitchen*

**Jeremy** But I'm quite prepared to settle for sardines, biscuits and chocolate sauce!
**Celia** Well I'm not! A civilized meal is what I said, Jeremy, and a civilized meal we shall have. There's just time for me to go to the grocer's, and you to go to the farm shop.
**Jeremy** Celia ...
**Celia** (*fighting him off*) The sooner we're there, the sooner we'll be back ... (*meaningfully*) ... and the sooner we're back ...!
**Jeremy** Right. Farm shop. Right.

*Celia and Jeremy exit through the front door*

*Almost immediately, Sara enters from the bedroom—pursued by Humphrey*

**Sara** It's no good, Humphrey, I just cannot unpack my more intimate garments while you are standing there *ogling!*
**Humphrey** I was not ogling.
**Sara** You were—ogling. *And* ooing and ahhing.
**Humphrey** I was not ooing and ahhing.
**Sara** Unless you suffer from asthma, you were ooing and ahhing.
**Humphrey** But hang it all, I'm going to see your more intimate garments eventually.
**Sara** *You are most certainly not!* (*A pause*) We shall draw the curtains.
**Humphrey** Ahh!
**Sara** You're doing it again.
**Humphrey** I've done something much worse than that.

**Sara** What?

**Humphrey** *Ogling* your intimate garments. (*He produces the package*) For you. And, as you will see . . . for me too.

*Sara is intrigued—she undoes the package—and produces stockings and suspenders*

**Sara** Humphrey!

**Humphrey** Darling.

**Sara** Stockings and suspenders! I couldn't possibly wear them.

**Humphrey** Oh, but you must.

**Sara** I couldn't. I couldn't. But if I *do*—you must promise me you'll never tell Peregrine.

**Humphrey** I wasn't planning to.

**Sara** I'm afraid poor Peregrine wouldn't understand. You see, he doesn't realize that women can be as . . . as passionate as men! I suppose that's why I'm attracted to you. *You* know.

**Humphrey** I do. I do.

**Sara** I know. But Peregrine now . . . Do you know that once—a long time ago . . . I sent for a "Sex Kitten Play Suit".

**Humphrey** Get away!?

**Sara** I did. A "Sex Kitten Play Suit" in gold lamé. Mind you, it was very shoddily made—I found it had all sorts of holes in the most extraordinary places. Anyway, I put it on one night . . . and then *loomed* over Peregrine . . . and swung my tail at him. It had a tail you see . . . in mock mink. *Anyway*—no more than three swings and he opened his eyes, and got all sort of glazed-looking . . . transfixed with shock. I slipped away and put on my winceyette pyjamas again and from that day to this, he's never mentioned it . . . Thank goodness.

**Humphrey** Why "thank goodness"?

**Sara** Well, it would be so awful if anyone knew that one had such a lustful streak . . . especially one's own husband!

**Humphrey** Now *I* know. Mind you, I've always suspected.

**Sara** Really?

**Humphrey** Still waters run deep—fires down below, that sort of thing. How about that drink now?

**Sara** I'm not much of a drinker—especially at this time of the day . . . but don't let me stop you. If you feel you need one . . .

**Humphrey** (*quickly—his virility in question*) Me, no. Definitely no. So . . . what shall we do then . . . eh? Eh?

**Sara** Well. I *am* feeling more relaxed . . .

**Humphrey** And time we got to know each other a bit better, eh? Eh!?

**Sara** There *is* an irresistible quality about you.

**Humphrey** Irresistible, eh? Eh!? Shall we go? (*He starts to lead her up the stairs again*) A Sex Kitten Play Suit? Pity you didn't bring it with you.

**Sara** I didn't say I hadn't. Did I?

**Humphrey** (*can't believe his luck*) With all sorts of holes in extraordinary places?

**Sara** No, of course not. I had them invisibly mended.

*They exit into the bedroom. A pause—then suddenly the bedroom door opens again—Sara emerges, with Humphrey in pursuit*

**Humphrey** What did I do? What did I do?

**Sara** Nothing. I just want to make myself pretty for you, that's all. (*She opens the bathroom door*)

**Humphrey** But you look terrific as it is.

**Sara** I'll only be fifteen minutes or so.

**Humphrey** Fifteen minutes!?

**Sara** Half an hour at the most. Now you just relax and think nice thoughts.

*She exits into the bathroom. Almost immediately we hear Sara scream, and she comes rushing out of the bathroom again*

**Humphrey** Darling . . . ?

**Sara** There's a dead man in the bath!

**Humphrey** What?!

**Sara** Lying in the bath—face up—he looks horrible . . .

*Syd Clancy enters from the bathroom. He is about fifty, wears workmen's overalls and, as we shall see, he likes a little tipple—frequently. He is never drunk—but never actually completely sober either*

That's him—that's the dead man!

**Syd** Oh, you did give me a start!

**Sara** *I* gave *you* a start!

**Humphrey** What the devil were you doing lying in the bath?

**Syd** Looking up the tap, of course.

**Humphrey** Looking up the . . . ?! Who are you, what are you doing here?

**Syd** I'm Syd. Syd Clancy. My missis does the cleaning here . . . and I've just been fixing a new tap washer. I didn't expect there to be anyone else here.

*He is staring at them—and now Humphrey quickly clears his throat*

**Humphrey** Er . . . we're friends of the Winthrops.

**Syd** Oh. Well I'll be out of your way soon as I've put the water back on . . . (*He takes out a flask, swigs from it—then becomes aware of them staring at him, and explains*) Gave me a proper turn you did—brought on my nerves. (*He starts down the stairs*) Won't disturb you again—bathroom's all yours.

*Syd goes down the stairs—and exits into the cellar*

**Sara** (*a rising panic*) Humphrey——!?

**Humphrey** (*interjecting*) This doesn't change anything.

**Sara** But he's seen us.

**Humphrey** Exactly, so what have we got to gain by running away now? Besides, you heard him, he'll be gone in a couple of minutes . . .

**Sara** But——

**Humphrey** And if I'm any judge the man's half-cut—probably won't remember us anyway.

**Sara** (*regarding him, then capitulating*) Oh, Humphrey, I feel so safe with you.

**Humphrey** Shouldn't rely on that.
**Sara** Naughty. I'll be quick as I can.

*Sara exits into the bathroom*

*Humphrey remains a moment on the landing*

**Humphrey** I'll go out for a stroll.

*Sara half opens the door to peer out*

**Sara** What?
**Humphrey** Just going out for a stroll.
**Sara** Right.

*Sara exits into the bathroom*

**Humphrey** *May* help to relax me.

*The bathroom door opens, Sara looks out again*

**Sara** What? I couldn't hear you.
**Humphrey** Yes. They knew how to build these old houses . . . (*He raps the door with his knuckles*) Soundproof . . . once the door is shut . . . ! (*He likes the thought*) Yes . . . *yes!*
**Sara** Humphrey, I'm not sure you *are* thinking nice thoughts.
**Humphrey** I am. I will.

*Sara exits into the bathroom*

(*Starting down the stairs*) Nice thoughts now, Humphrey. Nice thoughts . . . If you see any birds or bees look the other way.

*He exits through the french doors into the garden, leaving the door open behind him*

*Almost immediately, we hear the key in the lock—the front door opens and Thelma Jessel enters. She is about thirty-five–forty, a bright, extrovert woman—well aware of her own sexuality and prepared to do something about it. Often! She has a mink carelessly tossed across her shoulders, and exudes self-confidence. She enters the area, tosses the coat aside, then surveys the area—she sees the chocolate box and takes one*

**Thelma** Mmm . . . Chocolate creams . . . Oh, do come on, Peregrine!

*Peregrine Ward enters, carrying two small overnight cases. He is about forty–forty-five, not unattractive if you could separate him from his discreet, matching waistcoat, City-type suit, plastered down haircut and clerical air. There is a furtive, wary air about him*

*Note: During the ensuing scene we may see Humphrey from time to time—as he prowls the garden beyond the french doors. He will remain unaware of Thelma and Peregrine, and they of him*

**Peregrine** I was just checking that we *are* alone here.

**Thelma** Of course we're alone. You know very well that the Winthrops don't return from honeymoon until *next* weekend. Why do we have to go through all this cloak and dagger stuff . . . ?

**Peregrine** We can't be too careful, Thelma.

**Thelma** But I do think it was excessive to dismiss the taxi three minutes after we got into it . . . and make us walk half a mile.

**Peregrine** I didn't like the way the driver looked at us.

**Thelma** You probably aroused his suspicions by refusing to tell him where we were actually going. Taxi drivers tend to deal in firm destinations.

**Peregrine** Inconclusive.

**Thelma** What?

**Peregrine** In a court of law, his evidence would be regarded as a personal judgement and therefore (*a glint of triumph*) . . . inadmissible.

**Thelma** Perhaps I shouldn't have kissed you as passionately as I did.

**Peregrine** (*brightening*) Yes, you did, didn't you? (*Reprovingly*) Have to watch that, Thelma.

**Thelma** But not here, surely . . . ? Not with the door firmly closed . . . ? (*She closes the door firmly behind her—then moves to kiss Peregrine*)

**Peregrine** (*eventually breaking free*) As a solicitor I am well aware of these things.

**Thelma** (*another kiss*) I'm sure.

**Peregrine** That taxi driver could not *swear* he saw us enter here together— and I of course would totally deny it.

**Thelma** Yes. (*A thought*) But wouldn't that be perjury?

**Peregrine** Also be bloody good sense, wouldn't it? I mean, you don't want to hurt Humphrey, do you? And I most certainly do not want to hurt Sara.

**Thelma** Darling, they're both miles away from here.

**Peregrine** (*grinning*) Yes.

**Thelma** (*regarding him*) I think that's why I'm so attracted to you . . .

**Peregrine** Sara's lack of proximity?

**Thelma** Your naughty boy quality . . . it's . . . refreshing somehow . . .

**Peregrine** I intend to be even naughtier.

*This time, more relaxed. He kisses her—they sink on to the sofa—he strokes her skirt-clad thigh*

My God!

**Thelma** What's wrong?

**Peregrine** Suspenders. I feel suspenders . . . and where there are suspenders, there are stockings . . . !

**Thelma** Excite you, do they?

**Peregrine** Excite me!? Oh, my darling, I can confess to *you* . . . if there's anything that really brings out the deep, lascivious passions within me, it's——

**Thelma** (*interjecting*) Doesn't Sara wear them for you?

**Peregrine** Sara!? (*He laughs*) Sara. I wouldn't know how to ask her. *Sara!?* I sometimes think that if I hadn't married her, she might have entered a nunnery.

*Carried away, he embraces Thelma, and they sink on to the sofa—and out of
sight of the landing*

*The bathroom door opens—Sara emerges, wearing a robe, but then,
thinking herself alone, her fantasies overtake her normal, natural reticence.
She pulls the robe aside to reveal stockings and suspenders, et al—does a
small, brief bumps and grinds routine—then, ready for action, exits into the
bedroom*

*Peregrine abruptly breaks the embrace and stands up*

I don't intend rushing anything.
**Thelma** Oh ...
**Peregrine** No, we have a whole, blissful weekend ahead of us ... so why
rush? Now, then, what about a drink? (*He picks up Humphrey's champagne*)
**Thelma** But that belongs to Winthrop.
**Peregrine** You were there when he made his magnanimous offer ... "Use
the place as your own" ...
**Thelma** I rather think he meant *you* and Sara—or *me* and Humphrey ...
**Peregrine** Probably. Anyway, Humphrey must have given him this ...
**Thelma** Oh?
**Peregrine** Yes, it's that favourite rare vintage of his. And, as Humphrey and
I are partners, it virtually belongs to me too ...
**Thelma** And so does his wife ... for a while anyway.
**Peregrine** (*looking at her*) Yes. Funny, I don't feel any twinge of conscience
at all.
**Thelma** Not even where Sara's concerned?
**Peregrine** Well, perhaps just a tiny bit. You know—stockings and suspenders sort of sums it up—the fact I can't ask her. I had a dream once—
particularly vivid ... Sara entered the bedroom wearing some kind of cat
suit ... very tight ... and obviously very old because it was full of holes.
As I recall, she waggled her tail at me ... provocatively ...
**Thelma** And then?
**Peregrine** I woke up and found Sara beside me—wearing the same old
winceyette. Ah ... not like you and Humphrey, eh?
**Thelma** What do you know about me and Humphrey?
**Peregrine** More than you think.
**Thelma** Oh? (*She sits up, regards him*) You mean he talks about ... us?
**Peregrine** Doesn't have to. I *know*. Those times when he comes into the
office ... a spring in his step ... *smiling. I know.*
**Thelma** Know what?
**Peregrine** Well ... *you* know.
**Thelma** A spring in his step sounds like new shoes ... and as for that silly
grin of his, it's a permanent fixture.
**Peregrine** No, no, I mean that "special look" that tells me ...
**Thelma** Tells you what?
**Peregrine** That you and he have recently. *You* know!

*During this exchange, we see Humphrey go past the french windows,
grinning, a skip in his step!*

**Thelma** Oh. (*She understands now*) Oh. (*She ponders it*) Really?
**Peregrine** Yes.
**Thelma** You can definitely tell?
**Peregrine** Absolutely.
**Thelma** Oh. (*She ponders it*) Can you tell exactly when?
**Peregrine** Not to the exact minute, no!
**Thelma** But you *can* tell?
**Peregrine** Yes!
**Thelma** It really shows?
**Peregrine** Yes, it really shows! Now can we please drop the subject!
**Thelma** Perry darling, you're jealous.
**Peregrine** Envious. For a couple who have been married as long as you
    have, the frequency sometimes seems slightly indecent!
**Thelma** (*placating*) Perry. You may have been wrong occasionally, you
    know.
**Peregrine** Eh?
**Thelma** At least a *few* of the times it might have been new shoes.
**Peregrine** (*grim*) Not last Thursday it wasn't. He was like a Cheshire cat . . .
**Thelma** Oh, Perry, let's not think about it any more . . . (*A sudden thought*)
    Last Thursday!?
**Peregrine** Yes.
**Thelma** But I didn't see Humphrey last Thursday—or the night before.
**Peregrine** What?
**Thelma** Don't you remember, I went to Bristol to set up my alibi for this
    weekend!?
**Peregrine** Did you?
**Thelma** You *know* I did. It was your idea. So, if last Thursday, Humphrey
    looked as though he'd recently . . . then the question is—where—when—
    and with whom?! The spring in his step doesn't ever hint at an identity,
    does it?
**Peregrine** Now let's not jump to conclusions. I may have been quite wrong.
    It could *easily* have been new shoes.
**Thelma** *And the smile?*
**Peregrine** Well . . . I . . . I may have told him a joke!
**Thelma** Peregrine, I am being serious!
**Peregrine** (*defensive*) I know some jokes. I know . . . well . . . I know at least
    five. One is quite funny—involving as it does, a one-legged Irishman, a
    deaf dog and——
**Thelma** (*interjecting*) Peregrine!
**Peregrine** (*quickly*) Anyway, come to think of it, I'm not at all sure it *was*
    last Thursday. No, it could easily have been the Thursday before. Or the
    *Tuesday* even. Yes, that's it. I obviously made a mistake.
**Thelma** You? You're such a stickler for detail—you never make mistakes.
**Peregrine** I'm beginning to think I have.
**Thelma** What?

**Peregrine** I thought the object of coming here was to spend some precious time together ... but you insist on wasting it discussing Humphrey's possible indiscretions.
**Thelma** Well, I *am* interested ... after all, I am his wife ...
**Peregrine** No!

*She reacts*

This weekend you are no longer Humphrey's wife—you are my woman.
**Thelma** Perry! What a thrilling thing to say. And you looked all sort of "cave-man" when you said it.
**Peregrine** Darling.

*They kiss and embrace—then Thelma breaks for a moment*

**Thelma** Anyway, it probably *was* new shoes.

*They embrace again. Then part—a bit breathless*

**Peregrine** Now—shall we have that drink?
**Thelma** Later. When we have something to celebrate.

*They both look up the stairs—then Peregrine moves to pick up the suitcases and now notices the open french doors*

**Peregrine** Typical Winthrop. (*He starts to close and lock the french doors*) Goes away on honeymoon, carefully locks the front door, and leaves his french windows wide open.
**Thelma** (*wickedly*) He probably had his mind on other things.
**Peregrine** Yes. Yes.

*Picking up the suitcases, they now ascend the stairs, then stop before the two bedroom doors*

**Thelma** Any particular choice?
**Peregrine** I always vote Conservative.

*Thelma and Peregrine enter the right-hand bedroom*

*As the door closes—Humphrey appears at the french doors and tries them— they are locked. He raps on them, shouts "Sara" (mouths it because we cannot hear him). Finally, resigned to the fact they are locked, he exits in the direction of the front door*

*As soon as Humphrey goes—so the right bedroom door opens—and Peregrine plunges out, flourishing the key. Thelma appears at the door after him*

**Thelma** Peregrine, leave it until later.
**Peregrine** No, no, Winthrop was quite adamant about it ... "Use the place as your own ... but make sure you put the key back." (*He sprints down the stairs, opens the front door, leans out to replace the key, returns, closes the door and runs back up the stairs*) From hereon, I'm all yours, darling.

*They exit into the bedroom—the door shuts*

*Immediately we hear the key go into the lock, the front door opens and Humphrey enters. He closes the door, walks forward, remembers the key in his hand, turns to open the door again, replaces the key, closes the door and then starts up the stairs. He rushes up to the left-hand bedroom, then stops dead—composes himself at a convenient mirror—THAT smile appears— and then, a spring in his step, he heads back to the bedroom door. He raps on it. No answer. He raps again—pause—then he tries the door—it is unlocked—he opens it—stares off-stage and . . .*

**Humphrey** (*breathlessly*) Oh my! Oh my darling . . . !

*He rushes in, closing the door behind him*

*Syd enters from the cellar door. He moves across the area to the front door. In his hand he carries a very strange piece of piping/plumbing*

**Syd** (*scathingly*) Made in Albania! Typical!

*Syd exits through the front door*

*The right-hand bedroom door opens and Thelma appears, now wearing a robe. She moves to enter the bathroom but at this moment Peregrine appears behind her*

**Thelma** I'll only be about ten minutes.
**Peregrine** There's no need to rush. Take twelve if you want to.

*Thelma turns and exits into the bathroom*

*Peregrine remains a moment*

No rush. No rush!

*He turns and dashes back into the bedroom, closing the door*

*Immediately the left-hand door opens and Humphrey enters, wearing a robe. He rushes down to pick up the champagne bottle, then runs up the stairs again—and as he exits back into the left-hand bedroom . . .*

*We hear the key go into the lock, the door opens and Jeremy and Celia enter, each carrying various groceries. He closes the door (having left the key outside as before)—then takes groceries from Celia, puts them down, then sweeps her up into his arms and starts to carry her up the stairs*

**Celia** Darling, no—I've told you before . . . Darling! Jeremy! No! (*She wriggles out of his arms*) Darling, I'm hungry. I really am.
**Jeremy** So am I.
**Celia** For *food*. (*She taps his nose*) Control yourself . . .

*She starts down the stairs again, Jeremy pursuing her. She picks up the groceries*

First of all, we will have that quiet, civilized meal.
**Jeremy** And second!?

**Celia** Second—we will do the washing-up.

**Jeremy** Third then!?

**Celia** I'm going to want to take a bath . . .

**Jeremy** I'm not even placed!

**Celia** (*lovingly*) Darling, I do love you very, very much . . . and I want you too . . . but there is really no need to rush, is there?

**Jeremy** Isn't there?

**Celia** Of course there isn't. Nobody knows we're home a week early. So there'll be no interruptions, not even a phone call . . . just you and I in our own little love-nest . . .

**Jeremy** And not a Jessel or Ward in sight, thank goodness.

**Celia** Yes. (*Suddenly suspicious*) What do you mean?

**Jeremy** Oh. Nothing, darling.

**Celia** Jeremy, what-do-you-mean?

**Jeremy** Well, must confess, as we approached the front door I had the tiniest trepidation.

**Celia** Trepidation?

**Jeremy** You know we've just landed the plum of legally representing the Morals and Clean Living Group . . . ?

**Celia** Yes, you told me, but what does that have to do with——?

**Jeremy** (*interjecting*) How would you like to start married life as the Mrs Winthrop of Jessel, Ward and Winthrop?

**Celia** Jeremy—you've been promoted!?

**Jeremy** No, but the Morals and Clean Living Group is enormous—bigger than the Church Commission . . . properties all over the place . . . Jessel and Ward won't be able to handle it alone. They'll have to take on a new partner—perhaps even open a new office—it's going to take a great deal of organizing.

**Celia** Jeremy, you're the most wonderful organizer! The church fête, the end of season cricket match . . .

**Jeremy** Child's play compared with this. No, *this* will require an organizing genius . . . and they've been looking in my direction.

**Celia** Oh, Jeremy.

**Jeremy** That's why I invited them down.

**Celia** Fine. (*Then*) Invited who down?

**Jeremy** The Wards and the Jessels. I told them at the wedding——

**Celia** (*interjecting*) You told them what?!

**Jeremy** I just happened to mention that . . . if either . . . or both of them fancied a day or two in the country while we were away . . . they could use the place as their own . . .

**Celia** You mean we could have come back to a full house?

**Jeremy** But we weren't *supposed* to come back.

**Celia** That's beside the point. I could have walked in here and found four house guests . . .

**Jeremy** No, darling—two *employers*. Under an obligation to me . . . anyway it didn't happen . . . and we *are* alone . . . (*He regards her*)

**Celia** (*considering then liking it*) The Mrs Winthrop of Jessel, Ward and Winthrop . . . ?

**Jeremy** But you're not Mrs Winthrop yet.
**Celia** I most certainly am.
**Jeremy** In name only. We still haven't.

*He kisses her—this time she accepts a bit. They breathlessly break for a moment*

Oh, Celia . . .
**Celia** Oh, Jeremy . . .

*They kiss again then break*

They *won't* turn up, will they?
**Jeremy** No, no, if they were coming, they'd be here by now . . .

*They kiss again—then Celia breaks it*

**Celia** Food.
**Jeremy** (*kissing her*) Delicious.
**Celia** *Food.* (*She gently pushes him away*) Let's get on with it.
**Jeremy** I am. I am.
**Celia** Our meal, Jeremy. Anyway, I don't want to be just grabbed . . . well, I do, but . . .

*Jeremy moves in again*

(*Quickly*) . . . softly, romantically . . . *and definitely after dinner.*

*She turns and moves back towards the kitchen. He follows her. They exit into the kitchen. As the door closes . . .*

*The bathroom door opens—Thelma enters, a robe around her. She moves to the bedroom door, opens it, then, her back to the audience, opens her robe wide to "flash" herself at Peregrine (off-stage, within the room). We hear Peregrine's strangled cry of passion—then Thelma enters the bedroom and closes the door behind her*

*The second bedroom door opens—Sara emerges, hugging a robe around her. She comes down the stairs, a kind of cool detachment about her*

*Humphrey appears at the door, pulling on a robe as he hurries down after her*

**Humphrey** Sara . . . Darling?

*Sara moves to open a cigarette box, selects and lights a cigarette. Humphrey, puzzled by her attitude, moves closer*

Sara? Why are we down here?
**Sara** I wanted a cigarette.
**Humphrey** But I have some upstairs.
**Sara** I wanted a cigarette *down here.* I want to think . . .
**Humphrey** But, Sara—
**Sara** (*putting up a hand, interjecting*) Please, Humphrey, I'm thinking.

*He stares at her, as she paces the room a bit, then suddenly turns on him*

I think you should be thinking too, Humphrey.
**Humphrey** Thinking? What about?

**Sara** What you said to me up there a few moments ago.
**Humphrey** *I* said?! (*He frowns*) I said I loved you.
**Sara** Oh, no, you said more than that—"I love you, Sara, I love you . . . tell me you love me."
**Humphrey** What's wrong with that?
**Sara** Everything.
**Humphrey** What?!
**Sara** "I love you, Sara." You don't love me, Humphrey.
**Humphrey** But of course I do——
**Sara** (*overriding*) Then obviously you will want to use the phone.
**Humphrey** Eh?
**Sara** You will want to call Thelma . . . and ask her for a divorce.
**Humphrey** Oh, now . . . steady on . . .
**Sara** But you said you *loved* me.
**Humphrey** Yes, but when I said I loved you . . . I didn't mean . . . What I meant was . . . (*Blurting*) I always say that!
**Sara** And do you always say . . . "Tell me you love me?"
**Humphrey** Well . . . well, I'm not the most original thinker.
**Sara** I couldn't possibly, Humphrey.
**Humphrey** Possibly what?
**Sara** Tell you that I loved you. It wouldn't be true . . . any more than your declaration of love for me.
**Humphrey** Sara . . . Darling . . .
**Sara** *I* love Peregrine. And, I suspect, in your own funny way, *you* love Thelma.
**Humphrey** Well, I . . . I'm very *fond* of her——
**Sara** (*interjecting*) Exactly. So this digression into talk of love is ridiculous. I also find it very off-putting.
**Humphrey** I'm sorry . . . I didn't know.
**Sara** Well, you know now.
**Humphrey** Would it help if I said I don't love you?
**Sara** That's better. Much better.
**Humphrey** How about a modicum of affection?
**Sara** That is perfectly acceptable . . . and quite practical for our purpose. Yes, under these circumstances, affection is not only acceptable, but desirable.
**Humphrey** (*brightening*) How do you feel about passion?
**Sara** I'm all for it. As long as it's lust—not love.
**Humphrey** I think I can manage that.
**Sara** Good. We are beginning to understand one another. You see, Humphrey, I didn't rush into this affair headlong.
**Humphrey** Really?
**Sara** Indeed no . . . I gave it a great deal of thought. I considered my deep and real feelings for Peregrine . . . then decided it would be good for him.
**Humphrey** What!?
**Sara** For our marriage. To dissipate the carnal desires that you and I have been building up over these past few months. To burst the bubble. Beautifully.

**Humphrey** I say, what a charming way of putting it. So, now that we have firmly established that I do not love you, and you do not love me, shall we go back to bed and make love!?

*Sara and Humphrey ascend the stairs, exit into the bedroom and close the door. (Note: Sara leaves her lighter behind)*

*The kitchen door opens—Celia appears with Jeremy pursuing her. She moves to open the sideboard—and takes out some plates. Jeremy tries to embrace her*

**Celia** Darling, at this rate, I'll never get the dinner ready.
**Jeremy** Just one kiss . . . on the strength of my new partnership.
**Celia** You haven't got it yet.
**Jeremy** Oh, but I will—once I've got *us* organized.

*Celia relents—they kiss*

*And during this, the front door opens and through it comes a length of pipe. This should be as long as possible and* practicable. *The impression is of endless pipe entering the door. Then, at the end of the pipe, Syd enters*

*Celia and Jeremy are transfixed*

**Jeremy** Mr Clancy!
**Syd** Mr Winthrop! Oh, this is a disappointment—I was hoping to surprise you.
**Celia** What makes you think you didn't?!
**Syd** No, I mean you're home early—I was just fixing the tap for you.

*They stare at him*

The tap in the bathroom that's always dripping. Found the trouble—just a washer required that's all.
**Jeremy** (*staring at the length of pipe*) A washer!?
**Syd** Oh, I've fixed *that*. But when I come to put the water back on I found another little bit of trouble.
**Jeremy** Trouble?
**Syd** In the cellar. But don't you go worrying yourself—Simple enough for a man of my experience . . . I'll have it fixed and be out from under your feet in a couple of minutes.
**Jeremy** That's awfully kind of you.
**Syd** Think nothing of it. You're very good to my missis and I said . . . "If I can save Mr Winthrop a bit of trouble *and* money into the bargain" . . .
**Jeremy** Very kind—would you like a drink?
**Syd** Well, Mr Winthrop, you know I don't usually . . . but just lately my nerves *have* been brought on and . . .
**Jeremy** Help yourself.
**Syd** Thank you.

*Syd hands Jeremy the pipe, then picks up a bottle and charges his flask with it. Jeremy and Celia react.*

There weren't no Albanians living in this house before you were there?
**Jeremy** Albanians!?
**Syd** No, well I just wondered. You're a lucky man, Mr Winthrop.
**Jeremy** (*embracing Celia*) I think so.
**Syd** Got here in the nick I did. In the very nick. That leaking tap could 'ave
escalated something terrible. Nasty situation in that cellar of yours . . .
**Celia** Nasty . . .!?
**Syd** Don't you fret yourself, Mrs Winthrop—Syd'll fix it. All under control.
(*He recorks and pockets the flask then pours himself a glass of liquor*) 'Ave
it all fixed up in a couple of ticks. Cheers. Well. (*He takes the pipe from
Jeremy*) Thanks for the drink.

*Syd, with his pipe, exits into the cellar—he goes first—so that the long pipe
trails behind him—taking some time to disappear—and finally the door
shuts the two of them from sight*

*Jeremy looks at Celia*

**Jeremy** It *is* very kind of him.
**Celia** For a "little trouble" he seems to have an awful lot of pipe.
**Jeremy** Experienced workman. You could tell that—prepared for anything.
**Celia** Right—dinner.

*Celia exits back into the kitchen—Jeremy follows her*

*The bedroom door opens—Peregrine appears, comes downstairs to sit on
the sofa, and puts his head in his hands*

*Thelma appears at the bedroom door, pulling on her robe*

**Thelma** Perry?

*He does not move—she comes down the stairs to him, and during the ensuing
scene, will eat at least one chocolate cream*

Perry?
**Peregrine** (*head in hands*) This has never happened to me before. I feel so
ashamed . . . so . . . inadequate.
**Thelma** But you were doing so well, darling.
**Peregrine** I'm not usually like this.
**Thelma** (*comfortingly*) Of course you're not.
**Peregrine** Do you think it could be the first signs of senility?
**Thelma** *Darling.* Everything's going to be all right, I promise you. Now,
let's go back to bed and——
**Peregrine** (*interjecting*) I'm making excuses, when I know full well what it
was.

*She reacts as he turns to look at her*

We've been up there, tasting the delights of an illicit affair . . . and not
once have we said we love each other! I need an emotional involvement,
Thelma . . . Even if only for a brief weekend . . . I can't *function* without
emotion.

**Thelma** But, my darling Perry . . . I *do* love you.
**Peregrine** What?
**Thelma** I love you very, very much.
**Peregrine** (*brightening*) Really?
**Thelma** Really. And you know how you love me.
**Peregrine** By George, I think you're right . . .
**Thelma** Perhaps we should go back to the bedroom now?
**Peregrine** Love. Yes, I honestly think it *is* love. Yes. *Yes.* Oh, my darling
Thelma . . . I love you, I love you, I love you . . .

*They kiss. They part*

**Thelma** Then why are we standing around down here!?

*Grabbing his hand, she hurries him back up the stairs and into the bedroom.
As the door closes . . .*

*The kitchen door opens—Jeremy enters and goes to the sideboard drawers*

**Jeremy** Napkins . . . Napkins . . . (*He starts to search for and find napkins*)

*During this action, the bedroom door opens, Humphrey appears and hurries
down to where Sara has left her lighter. He picks it up. Now Jeremy sees
him—reacts—dumbstruck for a moment as Humphrey flicks the lighter on
and off*

**Humphrey** I love her. I love her not, I love her. I love her not . . . Oh my
God—Winthrop! Winthrop, what are you doing here?
**Jeremy** I live here, sir.
**Humphrey** I know that, but you're not supposed to be back until next week.
**Jeremy** I know sir . . . but it's a long story. (*Recovering rapidly*) Oh, but it
doesn't have to change anything.
**Humphrey** Not for you perhaps.
**Jeremy** (*continuing*) I'm delighted you decided to take me up on my
invitation . . . absolutely delighted, sir . . . and Celia will be too, sir. And of
course you'll stay the night, and both of you must join us for dinner.
**Humphrey** Both?
**Jeremy** Well, I imagine you brought Mrs Jessel with you?
**Humphrey** Ah . . . well . . . as a matter of fact, Winthrop——

*At this moment Sara appears at the bedroom door, holding an unlit cigarette*

**Sara** Humphrey, darling . . . I'm waiting for you to light my . . . (*she sees
Jeremy*) . . . my . . . my . . . my God!
**Jeremy** (*seeing Sara*) *Mrs Ward!*
**Humphrey** (*quickly*) Don't worry darling . . . I'll take care of this . . . after
all, Winthrop is married now . . . a man of the world . . . aren't you,
Winthrop?
**Jeremy** (*stunned*) Am I sir!?
**Humphrey** (*to Sara*) Go back and wait for me. Go on.

*Sara, in shock, retreats into the bedroom and closes the door*

**Humphrey** Now, Winthrop.

*Jeremy is still stunned*

*Winthrop!*
**Jeremy** Yes, sir ... sorry, sir ...
**Humphrey** Winthrop, I know how it appears ... I know what you're
thinking ...
**Jeremy** Oh, no, sir——
**Humphrey** (*overriding*) And you are absolutely right! Winthrop ... you
look rather pale ... shall we take a turn around the garden, while I
explain?

*He opens the french doors, starts to lead Jeremy out through them*

I think I should begin at the beginning ... with the vacancy for a
partnership in our company ...

*He closes the door behind them. They remain—seen through the french
doors—Humphrey talking volubly (unheard) to a Jeremy who is very
animated in his reactions*

*The kitchen door opens—Celia enters*

**Celia** Jeremy ... ? Jeremy! (*She sees the napkins lying on top of the
sideboard—frowns—starts to pick them up—and at this moment ...*)

*The bedroom door opens and Thelma hurries down the stairs to pick up the
box of chocolate creams. She is in a position where Humphrey and Jeremy
cannot see her—nor she them—but we can see all four players on stage*

**Celia** (*reacting*) Mrs Jessel!
**Thelma** (*breathing*) Oh my God! Celia! (*Then sharper*) What are you doing
here ... ?
**Celia** Well, it is my home now.
**Thelma** But you're not due back until next week.
**Celia** It's a long story. Oh, but you mustn't worry. Jeremy will be delighted
that you decided to take him up on his invitation ... you'll be staying the
night of course? ... And you must both join us for dinner.
**Thelma** Both?
**Celia** You and *Mr* Jessel of course. He *is* with you?
**Thelma** Well ... er ... as a matter of fact——

*At this moment Peregrine appears at the bedroom door*

**Peregrine** Thelma darling, how can you think about *chocolates* at a time
like this!?

*He and Celia see each other as one. He reacts as though struck by an invisible
fist*

**Celia** Mr Ward!
**Peregrine** (*calmly*) Good-afternoon, Celia. (*Then the utter panic*) Oh my
God! *Thelma ... what are we going to do*!?

**Thelma** Leave it to me, darling. After all, Celia is a married woman now . . .
I'll explain.
**Peregrine** But——
**Thelma** Just go back into the room and lie down.
**Peregrine** (*hoarsely*) Yes . . . yes . . .

*He retreats into the room, closing the door*

**Thelma** (*turning to Celia*) Celia dear, there *is* no explanation. It *is* what it
appears. Peregrine and I are having an affair. We just couldn't help
ourselves—we are so very, very desperately in love, you see. At least until
tomorrow. You're shocked?

*Celia tries to move—tries to speak—but only a vague sound emits*

Yes, I can see you're shocked. And it is awfully embarrassing that you
have found us out . . . under your own roof too . . . but we didn't expect
you back . . . and anyway . . . I'm sure there will be hidden advantages for
you and your husband. You *are* aware I suppose that there will shortly be
a vacancy in the partnership? And I am very influential with my husband
in that direction . . . and I happen to know that he will be looking for a
man of discretion, tact and integrity . . . in other words, someone who can
keep his mouth shut. Do we understand each other?
**Celia** (*finding her voice at last*) I . . . I think so.
**Thelma** I thought you would, Celia dear. After all, we're all adults in a
modern world, aren't we? Right. (*She retreats up the stairs. Entering the
bedroom*) We'll see you about eight then?

*Celia looks blank*

At dinner?

*She exits into the bedroom*

**Celia** Dinner . . . yes . . . (*Sudden thought*) Dinner!

*She turns and rushes off to exit into the kitchen*

*Jeremy and Humphrey enter through the french doors*

**Jeremy** Don't worry, sir . . . you can rely upon my integrity . . . *and* should
you see fit to consider me for the vacant partnership . . . ?
**Humphrey** What about your wife?
**Jeremy** You're not considering making *her* a partner too?
**Humphrey** No, no, I mean . . . (*He looks up at the bedroom*) How will she
take all this . . . ?
**Jeremy** Don't worry, sir . . . I'll explain everything . . . *she'll* understand.
Neither you or Mrs Ward need fear any hostility *or* embarrassment from
that quarter.
**Humphrey** (*staring up the stairs*) See you at dinner then . . . what time, by
the way?
**Jeremy** Oh . . . eight o'clock or thereabouts.
**Humphrey** Right.

*Humphrey enters the bedroom*

**Jeremy** Dinner ... gosh ... better warn Celia ... (*He turns towards the kitchen*)

*At this moment Celia hurries in to start looking in the sideboard*

(*Hesitating*) Darling ... I'm afraid we don't have the house to ourselves——

**Celia** (*working*) I know.

**Jeremy** (*continuing*)—no, I'm *not* afraid ... it's a fantastic stroke of good luck and ... (*Reacting*) You know! How could you know?

**Celia** (*waving up at the bedroom*) I've just seen her.

**Jeremy** Her? You mean Mrs——?

**Celia** (*interjecting*) She explained everything.

**Jeremy** And you understand? I mean—you don't mind?

**Celia** As you said, Jeremy, it is a fantastic stroke of good luck. She spoke about the partnership.

**Jeremy** *So did he!* My goodness, and here I was wondering how I'd break it to you ...

**Celia** Break what?

**Jeremy** Well, after all, they *are* having an illicit liaison ...

**Celia** Jeremy, we *are* all adults in a modern world ...

**Jeremy** Then you *really* don't mind?

**Celia** If I minded, would I have invited them to dinner?

**Jeremy** You did? So did I! (*He kisses her*) How could I have doubted you for one moment?

**Celia** Doubted?

**Jeremy** For one, silly, stupid moment, I was expecting trouble. Instead we are going to have a quiet, untrammelled dinner. Just the four of us.

CURTAIN

# ACT II

*Later that evening*

*When the* CURTAIN *rises, the lights are on, and outside it is already dusk. As the scene progresses, so it will get progressively darker. The stage is empty. The table is partially laid up for four*

> *The cellar opens and Syd enters carrying a piece of pipe. He is completely soaked to the skin—his damp overalls hang on him. Syd moves to pick up the phone and dials a number*

**Syd** (*on the phone*) Charley, Syd. Charley, I've got a little problem. . . . What's that? Hold on, my ear's full of water. (*He clears it—then:*) What? . . . Yes, that's right—water. . . . Well, that's the problem, Charley. I'm doing these folks a favour you see . . . Just tightening up the main inlet. . . . Yes. . . . Yes? Well—there's this nelly-box attached to a round thing, and a bit of pipe that goes off to the left. (*Listening then, patiently*) The left as I'm standing, Charley. . . . Yes. Oh, yes, I've located the up pipe and the down pipe—but then there's a bloody great *cross* pipe, made in Albania I shouldn't wonder. . . . *Albania*. (*Listening*) No, it isn't leaking, Charley. . . . No, that's no good, Charley. You see it's more pouring than leaking. Well, to be exact it's bloody gushing. (*Listening*) Yes Charley, I can swim. I'm asking you for a bit of help, Charley—like when I helped you put up that garden shed. (*Listening*) Well, you weren't supposed to *slam* the door, Charley . . . and nobody was hurt was they? (*Listening*) Well not *seriously*. Now what about this situation? . . . Yes? Put in a new pipe? Yes, I think I've got enough pipe for that. . . . Yes. . . . Yes. . . . Yes. . . . Thanks, Charley.

*He hangs up, then exits into the cellar again, taking another drink en route*

*Jeremy enters from the bedroom, calling back*

*Syd enters from the cellar and puts down his tool bag—reacting to Jeremy talking to himself*

**Jeremy** And you must call me Jeremy. Oh, yes, you already do . . . My organizing ability . . . ? (*Preening*) Oh, you may call it "genius" if you wish, but I modestly prefer to call it——
**Celia** (*off*) Jeremy!
**Jeremy** Yes, dear.

*Syd exits into the cellar again*

*Celia enters from the kitchen, carrying more things for the table*

**Celia** (*laying up more things*) Oh, Jeremy ... do get out of the way ... go
and get the wine or something.
**Jeremy** Right, darling.

*Jeremy exits into the kitchen*

*Celia finishes laying up, regards the table, then looks around her warily—and
then sits down at her place*

**Celia** Mrs Jessel ... Please call me Celia—oh yes, you already do! Well,
Thelma—you don't mind if *I* call you Thelma? I mean, as my husband is
so very much a part of Perry's *partnership* now ... (*She smiles*)

*During this, Syd enters from the cellar, to put down a large pipe wrench
alongside the pipe and tool bag—and again he stops to watch and listen to
Celia speaking to herself*

Yes, it *is* so well organized since you put your faith in him. Dare I say ...
better organized than ever before ... May I offer you another *petit four*
... ? (*She reacts*) Petits fours!

*Celia rises and hurriedly exits into the kitchen*

*Syd, bemused, stares after her and is about to pick up all his things*

*The bedroom door opens and Peregrine enters, dressed for dinner. He
descends the stairs, regards the table, then sits down*

**Peregrine** (*tentatively*) Jeremy. You don't mind if I call you Jeremy?
Jeremy, I would completely understand if you misinterpreted the situa-
tion—the fact that I have been sharing a bed with Mrs Jessel but I assure
you there is a perfectly rational explanation ... and I am still desperately
trying to think of it ... ! Furthermore ... furthermore ... (*Seeing Syd
watching him*) who are you!?
**Syd** Just a local craftsman, sir ... practising his craftsmanship.
**Peregrine** My God, how long have you been there ... how much did you
hear!?
**Syd** Don't you worry yourself—I do it a lot myself.
**Peregrine** I don't do it a lot!
**Syd** Well neither do I really ... (*winking*) ... only when there's no-one
around to see and hear. It clears the mind, don't it?
**Peregrine** The mind!?
**Syd** Oh, yes, talking to yourself ... you'd be surprised how many people do
it—especially around here. I find it a therapy. Mind you—I run up
against the same misunderstandings as I expect you do.
**Peregrine** Misunderstandings?
**Syd** Yes, a lot of people think *I'm* barmy too.

*Pipe and tools gathered up, Syd moves to the front door, and exits*

*The bedroom door opens. Thelma enters, dressed for dinner in blue with a
plunging neckline*

**Peregrine** This place is full of witnesses!

**Thelma** What?

**Peregrine** Oh, it's too late now, but I still think we should have packed up and left.

**Thelma** It wouldn't change the fact—they know.

**Peregrine** I feel so ashamed. Caught. *In flagrante delicto.*

**Thelma** There hasn't been much *flagrante* . . . and the *delicto* has been conspicuous by its absence.

**Peregrine** Winthrop coming back—it brought home to me just what we are doing.

**Thelma** Doing? We haven't done anything.

**Peregrine** What we were thinking of doing.

**Thelma** Oh, Perry. You spoke in the past tense. Does that mean that you've stopped thinking of doing?

**Peregrine** Well, no . . . yes . . . no, not really . . . What I mean is, I haven't gone off you . . .

**Thelma** Probably because you haven't got on me yet.

**Peregrine** I just wish I could get Humphrey out of my mind.

**Thelma** I've got him out of mine—why should you have any problem?

**Peregrine** It's . . . it's what I'm doing to him . . .

**Thelma** To him?

**Peregrine** Lusting after his wife . . . making mad passionate love to her . . .

**Thelma** Oh, good! When? . . .

**Peregrine** And then there's Sara. I do love her really, you know . . . and I've never been unfaithful before.

**Thelma** Your record remains untarnished.

**Peregrine** But tainted by my unquenchable desire for you.

**Thelma** Oh, I don't think completely unquenchable . . . You'll see . . . later on tonight. (*She subtly lifts her skirt to again display stockings and suspenders*)

**Peregrine** That's grossly unfair.

**Thelma** All's fair . . . in love . . .

*She caresses him again—he begins to respond*

**Peregrine** Thelma, don't do that.

*She continues*

Please don't do that.

**Thelma** Why?

**Peregrine** Because I like it so very desperately.

*They kiss, then break for a moment*

If only we could have discussed it with Sara and Humphrey . . . and perhaps got their permission?

*Thelma kisses him again—more deeply*

*Celia enters from the kitchen, carrying a bowl of* petits fours. *She stops*

*A beat—then Peregrine becomes aware of her—and disentangles himself rapidly*

Celia . . . !

**Celia** Good-evening.

**Peregrine** It isn't what you think. We were kissing—I admit—but not passionately.

**Thelma** I was.

**Peregrine** Celia, I . . . I'm still most acutely embarrassed by this whole situation.

**Celia** Please, you don't have to be—Jeremy and I understand perfectly.

**Peregrine** That's what's so embarrassing!

**Celia** Anyway, it's the most marvellous opportunity.

**Peregrine** Opportunity?

**Celia** (*at Thelma*) For Jeremy to prove to you that he is a man of discretion, tact and integrity.

**Thelma** (*at Celia*) We'll talk about it over dinner. When is dinner, by the way?

**Celia** Oh, not long. A quarter of an hour or so.

**Thelma** We have time for a stroll then . . . Perry?

*They move towards the french doors*

**Peregrine** Yes, a stroll in the air will perhaps help cool me down. (*He then reacts—and turns to Celia*) Oh, I didn't mean *that*. I didn't mean what it sounds like I meant. What I meant was——

**Thelma** (*interjecting*) Perry.

*She grabs his arm and they exit through the french doors*

*Celia turns back towards the kitchen*

*Jeremy enters from the kitchen, holding an uncorked bottle of wine aloft*

**Jeremy** A Château-Latour . . . it's a full-bodied, sensuous, breathing thing . . . which reminds me, darling—we don't want this dinner to go on too late, do we?

**Celia** It'll go on just as long as it takes to clinch your partnership. But, Jeremy, you must be very careful not to embarrass him.

**Jeremy** Embarrass him?

**Celia** He's very sensitive about the whole thing.

**Jeremy** Well, that's a bit late in the day. I mean, we've all suspected, if not known, that he's been playing around for years.

**Celia** What!? *Him*!? And I thought it was *she* who had led him on.

**Jeremy** What!? Her!? That shy little creature?

**Celia** (*regarding him*) Oh, Jeremy darling, you can be so naïve . . . (*She moves to the kitchen, then pauses*) "Shy little creature." In that plunging blue dress?! Must find out where she got it!

*Celia exits*

*Jeremy remains, a bit baffled. He moves to put the wine on the table*

*The bedroom door opens and Sara appears—her dress is NOT blue—and is buttoned demurely to the throat*

**Jeremy** (*regarding her*) Oh, you've changed. My wife will be disappointed.
**Sara** Oh! We thought we'd dress for dinner—but if it embarrasses you——
**Jeremy** (*interjecting*) No, no. The last thing I want to do is cause embarrassment. I've had specific instructions.
**Sara** (*a bit bemused*) Well, I actually popped out to tell you that we are going to be a bit late for dinner ... it's Humphrey ... a tiny accident ...

*Humphrey enters from the bedroom, and remains in the door, demonstrating a broken fly zip*

**Humphrey** Damned zip's broken ...
**Sara** Beyond repair ... and we were wondering, Jeremy ... you have some trousers in the wardrobe ... and I always carry a needle and thread with me ...
**Humphrey** Can we pinch one of your zips, old boy?
**Jeremy** Of course—feel free ...
**Humphrey** Thanks, old boy ...
**Jeremy** You're welcome and don't worry about being late ... I'll warn Celia.

*Humphrey and Sara exit into the bedroom again. The door closes*

*Celia enters from the kitchen to put out more things on the table*

**Celia** Won't be long now ...
**Jeremy** No rush. They're going to be a bit late.
**Celia** Oh, they're back then?
**Jeremy** (*frowning*) Back? Yes, they're upstairs in the bedroom.
**Celia** (*reacting*) What!?
**Jeremy** It's all right though—she's got his trousers off and they're at it now ... shouldn't take long.

*Celia stares at him*

(*Ingenuously explaining*) He had trouble with his zip you see ... I had to help him out.
**Celia** *Jeremy!*
**Jeremy** I'm sure you would have done the same under the circumstances ... anyway, not to worry, they'll be down again soon ... oh, and must warn you ... don't look too surprised when you see that she's taken the blue dress off.
**Celia** Jeremy, what kind of dinner party do you think this is going to be!?
**Jeremy** Oh, I hope informal ... intimate ...
**Celia** I absolutely refuse.
**Jeremy** What?
**Celia** Partnership or not ... I draw the line at intimacy ...
**Jeremy** Celia ... (*He is now positioned so that he can see out of the french doors and he now reacts*) Oh my God!

*Celia reacts*

*Mr* Ward and *Mrs* Jessel.

*Celia turns to look up at the bedroom*

No, no . . . they're in the garden heading this way.
**Celia** Oh, good. (*She smiles*) So you *were* just joking with me . . .

**Jeremy** They're coming in . . . and they're dressed for dinner!

*Peregrine and Thelma appear at the french doors and, as they move to enter*

**Celia** Well, what else would they be dressed for, Ah . . .

*As Peregrine and Thelma enter, Celia moves to greet them. Jeremy remains transfixed*

Your timing could not be more perfect . . . I am just about to serve . . .
Now, why don't you sit here . . . you here . . . and Jeremy will . . . (*She glances at Jeremy, sees his transfixed state*) Jeremy . . . ? *Jeremy!*
**Peregrine** Must have been a great shock to you when Celia explained about
. . . er . . . Mrs Jessel and I . . . I promise you, we were equally shocked . . .
when Thelma stepped out of the bedroom to find that you and Celia had
returned . . . Had we known . . . or even guessed that you might have
returned unexpectedly . . . we most certainly would not have used *your*
house for *our* rendezvous . . . and furthermore . . . (*He now becomes aware
of Jeremy's transfixed state and looks at Celia*) You *did* explain to him?
**Celia** I did. I have. Jeremy?
**Thelma** He looks awfully pale.
**Jeremy** It cannot go on! The feast Celia has prepared—it cannot go on—
without . . . without wine to go with it!
**Peregrine** ⎱
**Celia**      ⎰ (*together*) Wine?
**Thelma**   ⎰

*As one, they all look at the open bottle of wine on the table*

**Jeremy** Ah . . . oh . . . ee . . . oh . . . ah . . . (*He grabs up the bottle and a
napkin, spills wine on to a napkin and starts to polish the table with it*)
Furniture polish!
**Celia** Jeremy——
**Jeremy** (*overriding*) Yes . . . I wanted to finish this and have the table all
shiny and nice for you . . . furniture polish.
**Peregrine** It looks like a wine bottle to me.
**Thelma** And I can see a vintage printed on the label . . . nineteen sixty-seven
. . .
**Jeremy** Ah . . . no . . . one thousand nine hundred and sixty-seven known
germs . . . and this stuff copes with 'em all . . . right, darling . . . ?

*Celia opens an astonished mouth*

*Right!* I know it's an awful cheek and all that . . . but would you mind
popping down to the pub and buying a bottle . . . ? We don't have a drop
of wine left in the house . . .
**Celia** Jeremy, there are five more bottles in the cupboard.

**Jeremy** Of polish ... all of them polish ... I love polishing you see ... fanatical about it ...
**Celia** Jeremy.
**Jeremy** Please—or dinner will be a disaster!
**Peregrine** Well, if that's the case ... yes ... How do I get to this pub?
**Jeremy** Through the garden ... across the field ... over the foot-bridge ...
**Celia** But it's more than a mile away ...
**Jeremy** (*quickly*) Oh, no more than quarter of a mile, darling ...
**Peregrine** I'd better be off then. (*He moves to the french doors alone*)
**Jeremy** (*reaching for Thelma*) Oh, but you must take Mrs Jessel too ...

*They all stare at him*

In case you get lost. And you'll be company for each other ... anyway, if people see you apart so soon—they'll start talking!
**Peregrine** But we haven't been seen together yet.
**Jeremy** Exactly. This is your chance to still those malicious tongues!

*Peregrine is baffled, nevertheless, he looks at Thelma*

**Peregrine** He may have a point ...
**Thelma** Yes ...

*They move to the french doors—but Thelma pauses*

Are you *sure* dinner won't be ruined?
**Jeremy** Only if you stay ... (*He urges them out of the french doors*)

*Peregrine and Thelma exit*

*Jeremy turns—Celia is utterly astonished*

**Celia** Jeremy ...

*But he hurries past her, picks up the phone and starts dialling*

*Jeremy*! Have you taken leave of your senses? *Jeremy, what are you thinking of*!?
**Jeremy** Suicide! (*Into the phone*) Hallo ... *Rose and Crown*? ... May I have a word with Fred please? ... Thank you. ...
**Celia** Jeremy!
**Jeremy** Fred's account of World War Two must be good for at least an hour—mustn't it? Even if he only gives them the potted version ... ! (*Into the phone*) Fred? Jeremy Winthrop. ... Yes, I know D-Day must have been absolute agony. Fred ... FRED! (*Overriding the garrulous Fred*) Two friends of mine are popping over to the pub to buy some wine. ... No, I'm sure it doesn't compare with the wine from Armentières. ... Fred. ... FRED. These friends of mine are utterly fascinated by World War Two. Yes, Fred—I mean it. ... Yes, and no matter if they make excuses to leave—it's just their way of saying they want to hear more. And Fred—don't forget that phenomenal display of memory—the name *and* number of every man in your regiment. ... No, Fred—not to *me*, Fred— to *them*! (*He hangs up*)

**Celia** (*staring at him*) Jeremy, do you know what you've done!!?
**Jeremy** I've gained some time . . . precious time . . .
**Celia** *Jeremy, what is going on*!?
**Jeremy** Ward and Jessel are upstairs in the bedroom.
**Celia** Now I know you are insane. Ward and Jessel are on their way to the
pub!
**Jeremy** Not the pub Ward and Jessel. The *other* Ward and Jessel!
**Celia** (*staring at him, then*) It must have been the Spanish food.
**Jeremy** (*to himself almost*) I know now why she wasn't wearing the blue
dress with the plunging neckline. Because she never had it on!
**Celia** Jeremy, I think you'd better sit down. (*Genuine concern now*) What is
it, darling . . . have I put too much of a strain on you, denying you your
rights? (*She puts her arms around him*) Would it help if we do it now? Even
if Fred only gives them the potted version there's still lots of time!
**Jeremy** (*pulling free*) We've got enough of that going on around here
already!
**Celia** Jeremy . . .

*The bedroom door opens—Sara steps out on to the landing—with Humph-
rey entering from the bedroom too, remaining near the door*

(*Glancing at them, then double-taking*) Oh my God! (*And, like Jeremy
earlier, she becomes transfixed*)
**Sara** We've got the most awful confession.
**Humphrey** My fault. I went at it too hard.
**Sara** The fact is we took the zip out of your trousers, Jeremy, and now
*that's* broken too . . . Do you think we could . . . ?
**Jeremy** Not at all . . . use another pair . . .
**Sara** (*regarding Celia*) Celia looks awfully pale—is something wrong . . . ?
**Jeremy** It's the shock.
**Sara** Of course, foolish of me . . . it must have been a great shock to you
when Jeremy explained about . . . er . . . Humph . . . er . . . Mr Jessel and
me . . . but we are most awfully grateful at the way you are taking it . . .
aren't we, Humphrey?
**Humphrey** Oh, yes—awfully.

*Sara and Humphrey exit into the bedroom again*

*Celia starts to collapse—Jeremy catches her just in time*

**Jeremy** *Now* do you understand?

*Celia raises a shaking hand to point at the bedroom*

**Celia** Mr Jessel and Mrs Ward . . .

*Jeremy points at the french doors*

**Jeremy** And Mr Ward and Mrs Jessel . . .
**Celia** Oh my God.
**Jeremy** Amen.

*A pause—then:*

**Celia** When Mr Ward finds out about Mrs Ward and Mr Jessel . . .
**Jeremy** And when Mr Jessel finds out about Mrs Jessel and Mr Ward . . .
  disaster . . . of such magnitude Hollywood will probably want to film it!
**Celia** And worst of all, my first attempt at entertaining could lack the right
  party spirit.
**Jeremy** No, darling, there's something even worse than *that.*
**Celia** Impossible.
**Jeremy** The Morals and Clean Living Group.

*They stare at each other in horror*

**Celia** When *they* find out . . .
**Jeremy** That the company they've employed makes the Bacchanalian Rites
  look like a game of croquet . . .
**Celia** They'll withdraw.
**Jeremy** Taking my hopes of a partnership with them. And probably the job
  I *have* got with it.
**Celia** They couldn't—they wouldn't!?
**Jeremy** Be a great example of my organizing won't it!? Getting them all
  here to have it off at the same time!
**Celia** Jeremy, don't be crude.
**Jeremy** I'm being realistic. Do you know how many jobs I tried for after I
  left University? Do you know how many letters I wrote, doors I knocked
  on . . . *do you know what the mortgage on this place is?*!
**Celia** You told me it was part paid for.
**Jeremy** Yes. That part—about the door and the chimney. If I lose my job
  now . . . and that's what will happen. *They'll have to blame someone.* And
  goodbye job—money—home . . .
**Celia** Pitter patter of little Winthrops . . .
**Jeremy** It'll be the end of everything, darling. The bitter bloody end.

*A pause—then:*

**Celia** ⎫
**Jeremy** ⎰ (*together*) We can't let this happen!
**Celia** But it's going to. It's inevitable.
**Jeremy** Over the past few days I have learned that even the inevitable—
  isn't.
**Celia** Jeremy, this is hardly the time to be thinking of . . .
**Jeremy** I'm not. And you said it.
**Celia** Said what?
**Jeremy** We can't let this happen.
**Celia** You said it too.
**Jeremy** But with a touch more conviction.
**Celia** Jeremy, we have to face facts, the first duty of a host and hostess is to
  ensure that a man, his mistress *and* his wife are not seated at the same
  table . . . *and we'll be doing it twice!*
**Jeremy** Exactly.

*She stares at him*

Don't you see ... *two* dinner parties!?

*She still stares at him*

The other Ward and Jessel are off to the pub ... and with the grace of
God and Fred's memories of World War Two, they should be there for
more than an hour at the very least ...! Time enough for us to wine and
dine Jessel and Ward and pack them off to bed. They're bound to want to
go to bed early ... as a matter of fact, that was my intention—although
just now I can't remember why!

**Celia** (*staring at him*) Two dinner parties!?

**Jeremy** It's our only hope.

**Celia** Do you think we could get away with it?

**Jeremy** Well, they never found Jack the Ripper. Darling, we might get away
with it ... we just might.

**Celia** But they're all staying the night.

**Jeremy** We'll worry about that later ...

**Celia** (*considering*) It's mad—but it might work.

**Jeremy** It has to.

**Celia** Very well. Let's start the first sitting. (*She moves to the kitchen, then
pauses*) But, darling ... the chicken is really only big enough to feed four
... so if I ask you what you want ...

**Jeremy** Don't worry—I'll ask for beak!

*Celia exits*

*Jeremy hurries up the stairs and raps on the bedroom door*

*Sara opens the bedroom door and enters*

Don't want to rush you ... but dinner is about to be served.

**Sara** We'll be down in just a minute.

**Jeremy** Right.

*Sara exits into the bedroom*

*Jeremy turns to descend the stairs*

*At this moment Peregrine and Thelma enter through the french doors. They
are a bit dishevelled and muddy*

Oh my God!

**Peregrine** Don't be alarmed ... despite our dishevelled appearance, we are
unharmed ...

**Thelma** But we didn't get to the pub ... *or* get the wine ...

**Jeremy** Never mind, I'll polish the furniture with something else ...! We
didn't expect you back so soon ... what happened?

**Peregrine** We had an accident *en route* ... the footbridge ... it shouldn't be
allowed ...

*Jeremy starts to hustle them up the stairs*

**Thelma** (*proudly*) If Perry hadn't clasped me in his strong, masculine
arms ...

**Peregrine** It was a near thing, Winthrop ...

**Jeremy** Nearer than you think. I'm so sorry ... I've said a hundred times the council should do something about that bridge ... the boards are so slippery ...

**Peregrine** Slippery!? The damned thing just——

**Jeremy** (*overriding*) Obviously you must change your clothes ... (*As they both might speak*) Don't worry about dinner ... I'll tell Celia to delay it. I'll tell her there's been an unexpected development!

*Hustled by Jeremy, Peregrine and Thelma have ascended the stairs. They exit into the bedroom*

*Jeremy closes the door on them and remains, exhausted. He is then diverted as ...*

*The front door opens and Syd enters—he now carries a length of pipe about half the length of the earlier one. As he crosses to the cellar door, he waves up to Jeremy*

**Syd** It's all right for some, Mr Winthrop ... but it's all "go" for us workers.

*He exits into the cellar*

*Jeremy, bemused, leans his head against the Peregrine and Thelma door—regaining his wind and his senses*

*The other bedroom door opens—Humphrey and Sara enter and descend the stairs*

*Jeremy is unaware of them—and they of him. Humphrey and Sara glance around the empty area, then decide to sit down*

*Celia enters from the kitchen, carrying a bowl of croûtons*

**Celia** Won't be a moment now.

*Her voice causes Jeremy to react on the upstairs landing, and to turn and stare down at Humphrey and Sara seated and Celia just exiting into the kitchen*

*Celia exits*

**Jeremy** (*descending the stairs fast*) Furniture polish!

*Sara and Humphrey react*

**Sara**
      } (*together*) What!?
**Humphrey**

**Jeremy** In that bottle ... (*He snatches up the wine bottle*) Furniture bottle ... see!? (*He again upends the bottle on to a napkin and starts to polish all the furniture in sight*) There are five other bottles in the cellar.

**Humphrey** What?

**Jeremy** And none of them wine ... Oh God, and Celia's very first dinner party too ... and she was so anxious to get everything right ... and I haven't got a bottle of wine in the place.

**Sara** Oh dear.

**Humphrey** Well, surely there's a local pub . . .
**Jeremy** (*in a rush*) *The Rose and Crown* . . . just through the garden, across
the field . . . over the footbridge . . . but be careful the boards can be
awfully slippery! God, how I envy you, it's a lovely evening for a stroll . . .
**Humphrey** (*on his feet now*) Far, is it?
**Jeremy** I've known some people be there and back in five minutes!
**Humphrey** Well, dear . . . (*He regards Sara*) . . . we don't want to ruin
Celia's first dinner party, do we? Come along.
**Sara** You want me to come too . . . ?
**Humphrey** (*smiling wickedly*) Just in case I get lost.
**Jeremy** Oh, I am most awfully grateful . . . Mr Jessel.
**Humphrey** Call me Humphrey, Jeremy. You don't mind if I call you
Jeremy?

*They move to the french doors*

**Jeremy** Oh, just one more favour. The publican—his name's Fred. Would
you be so kind as to ask him about D-Day?
**Humphrey** D-Day?
**Jeremy** It's a private joke.
**Humphrey** D-Day? Very well.

*Humphrey and Sara exit through the french doors*

*Jeremy, close to utter exhaustion, follows them, to lean gratefully on the
french doors, watching them go*

*During this, the bedroom door opens. Peregrine and Thelma enter—come
down the stairs—and, unaware of Jeremy, move to regard the table—and
then they sit down*

*Celia enters from the kitchen, carrying a tray with four soup bowls on it*

**Celia** Now then . . . (*Seeing them—reacting*) Oh my God!

*This spins Jeremy around Peregrine and Thelma are shocked by Celia's
reaction—and the fact that she remains transfixed. He attempts to "cover" the
moment*

**Jeremy** She's obviously forgotten to put pepper in the vichyssoise. Isn't that
right, dear?
**Celia** (*still stunned*) They changed.
**Peregrine** Only our shoes. We didn't want to delay dinner.
**Jeremy** (*at Celia*) Don't worry, we've got an hour at least—even if it's only
the potted version.
**Peregrine** What?!
**Jeremy** Come along, darling . . . I'll help put it all right for you in the
kitchen . . .

*Taking the tray, he hustles Celia away.*

*They exit into the kitchen*

*A pause—then:*

**Peregrine** As a matter of fact I don't like pepper in my soup.
**Thelma** Don't be churlish, Perry. They're newly-weds anxious to make their
first dinner party a success. We mustn't spoil it for them.
**Peregrine** I still feel like an intruder.
**Thelma** It could have been worse. After all, Jeremy did invite all four of us
down here ... and could have come back and found both bedrooms
occupied ... and speaking of bedrooms ... (*She caresses his cheek*)

*Celia and Jeremy enter from the kitchen, Jeremy carrying the tray. Celia
will serve soup bowls from it as:*

**Celia** All's well—Jeremy explained everything ...
**Peregrine** Explained?
**Jeremy** (*hastily*) How to put the pepper in the soup!
**Peregrine** How to put the——?
**Thelma** (*interjecting*) Newly-weds, darling—newly-weds ...

*Celia sits down. Jeremy picks up the wine and starts to pour it. Peregrine and
Thelma react*

**Peregrine** (*clearing his throat*) Er ... Jeremy. You don't mind if I call you
Jeremy ...?
**Thelma** You already do, darling.
**Peregrine** Ah, yes ... well ... er ... Jeremy the wine.
**Jeremy** Oh, I'm sure you'll like it ... it's a very fine——(*He suddenly
realizes—and ends the sentence with a small strangled cry*) Oh, I see ... you
think it's furniture polish ... so did I ... Celia had mixed the bottles up,
hadn't you, darling ... (*Holding his glass aloft*) No, this is a superb little
claret ... it may be a bit on the young side, but it more than compensates
for that by its immaculate breeding ... it's robust without being bullying
... one can actually taste the grape and——
**Celia** (*interjecting*) Darling, we don't have all night you know.
**Jeremy** (*sitting down*) But we don't have to rush either ... say ... five
minutes on the soup ... fifteen on the main course ... the dessert ... or
cheese and biscuits ... coffee ... a brandy ... (*to Peregrine and Thelma*)
... you do drink brandy?
**Peregrine** (*puzzled*) Yes ...
**Jeremy** I'd say about forty-seven minutes overall ... gives us a safety
margin of thirteen minutes at least.
**Peregrine** A safety margin?
**Celia** For digestion.
**Peregrine** Oh. Yes, I understand.
**Celia** *Bon appétit.*

*They reply—start to eat their soup—a pause—then:*

**Peregrine** No. I don't understand. Is this some kind of race?
**Thelma** Darling, of *course* you understand.
**Peregrine** Do I?
**Thelma** They're newly-weds.
**Peregrine** Eh? Oh, yes, I see.

**Thelma** Which reminds me ... we haven't got *your* bedroom, have we?

**Celia** ⎫ (*together*) ⎧ Yes.
**Jeremy** ⎭            ⎨ No.

**Jeremy** Er ... what she means is ...

**Celia** What he means is ...

**Jeremy** We hadn't sorted out yet which *is* our bedroom.

**Celia** So you must stay exactly where you are.

**Peregrine** I'm getting embarrassed again.

**Jeremy** Please don't ...

**Peregrine** Apart from the circumstances, we are putting you to a lot of trouble.

**Jeremy** (*at Celia*) Trouble?

**Celia** Trouble?

**Jeremy** Perish the thought, we are absolutely delighted to have you here ... aren't we, darling?

**Celia** Hysterically happy!

**Peregrine** (*warmly*) I won't forget this weekend, Jeremy.

**Jeremy** I don't think we will either, sir.

**Thelma** Don't you think it's time he called you Peregrine, Peregrine?

**Peregrine** Peregrine Peregrine? Oh, yes ... see what you mean ... yes, please do, dear boy ... Yes. (*He picks up his glass*) We should drink to that ... to a new relationship ...

**Celia** I trust you mean business-wise too?

**Thelma** Of course he does.

*They drink*

**Peregrine** Mmm ... you were right about this claret, Jeremy ... not a hint of furniture polish about it ...

**Jeremy** Lucky—as you weren't able to get the wine.

**Peregrine** Yes, *we* were *very* lucky. Another couple of seconds and it wouldn't have been just our feet that got wet. Clear to see the bridge has been rotting away for years.

**Jeremy** Yes, I'm going to write to the council about it. One of these days that old bridge will collapse completely ...

**Peregrine** It did. Tonight.

**Jeremy** Just what I've been saying. (*He realizes*) What!?

**Peregrine** The bridge has gone.

**Thelma** It just fell into the river and broke into a hundred pieces.

**Jeremy** Gone!? (*At Celia*) That means that anyone who left here to go to the pub ...

**Celia** Will be back any minute!

*Jeremy gets to his feet and rushes to the french doors to stare out*

**Peregrine** You can't see the bridge from there.

**Jeremy** I know.

**Celia** What *can* you see?

**Jeremy** Nothing so far. (*He turns to regard the panicked Celia*)

**Celia** What are we going to do?!

**Jeremy** What are we going to do? . . .(*He rushes back to the table and starts to finish his soup at breakneck speed*) We're going to finish our soup . . . ! (*His soup finished, he pulls Peregrine's and Thelma's plates away from them and proceeds to load them on to the tray*) Right . . . right . . . And serve the next course on the patio . . .

**Celia** The patio!?

**Jeremy** You know, the concrete outside the kitchen . . .

*Celia is on her feet now—and he pushes the tray into her hand—and again runs over to the french doors to peer out*

It's a lovely balmy evening . . . and no-one in sight so far . . . (*He turns*) Yes, on the patio . . . in the summer air . . .

**Peregrine** It looked like rain to me.

**Jeremy** It can't rain. It mustn't . . . Please, God, don't let it *rain*! (*He starts to gather up various things from the table, handing them to Thelma and Peregrine*) Now you take that . . . you take those . . . I'll bring the glasses . . . and hurry.

**Peregrine** Hurry?

**Jeremy** Well, we are newly-weds!

**Peregrine** Ah, yes . . . hurry . . .

*Jeremy hustles Celia, Thelma and Peregrine out to the kitchen*

*Syd enters from the cellar, moves to pick up the phone and dials a number*

**Syd** (*on the phone*) Charley? Syd. That problem. . . . No, no better. In fact, and you know me, I'm never one to look on the dark side—but let's just say I know just how those poor unfortunate souls must have felt on the Titanic. (*He listens*) No, not before it sunk, Charley. After. (*He listens*) It's where the Albanian bit meets the good old British bit. Britain's losing. About thirty nil. . . . Well—you never seen a picture of the Niagara Falls? . . . A cross connection? Well, I'll try anything, Charley—but it ain't easy—water keeps putting my blowlamp out! (*During this conversation he quite naturally picks up the open bottle of wine and swigs from it*) This job's important, Charley because I reckon the whole house needs rewiring. (*He listens*) No, I haven't touched a single wire yet! But it's going to need doing . . . and if I make a good job of this one . . . (*He listens*) Thanks, Charley.

*He hangs up—takes another swig of wine—then moves back to exit into the cellar*

*Humphrey and Sara enter through the french doors. They react to the table, more or less denuded of everything save the wine bottle*

*At this moment Jeremy enters from the kitchen, rushes over to pick up the wine bottle—then reacts to the presence of Humphrey and Sara*

**Jeremy** Oh . . . ah . . . ah . . . I'm just polishing the kitchen chairs . . . do sit down . . .

**Humphrey** Jeremy, we weren't able to get to the pub and——
**Jeremy** (*overriding*) Dinner will be served immediately . . .

*Jeremy exits into the kitchen again*

*Humphrey and Sara are bewildered*

*A beat—then Jeremy enters from the kitchen again at a run, carrying cutlery and condiments. He dumps them down on the table*

Do you mind laying these up . . . ? Thanks. (*He turns to run out again*)
**Humphrey** Jeremy—the wine.
**Jeremy** Wine? Ah, yes.

*Jeremy exits into the kitchen—a beat—then Jeremy enters again, carrying a wine bottle and glasses—he rapidly pours three glasses*

**Humphrey** No—the wine *we* were going to get.
**Jeremy** Oh, I think you'll find this is much better.

*They stare as Jeremy pours the wine*

**Humphrey** We didn't get the wine because the bridge has collapsed.
**Jeremy** I know.
**Sara** You know?
**Jeremy** News travels fast in the country.

*He hands them their wine—they stare at it*

**Humphrey** Jeremy, we didn't *get* the wine.
**Jeremy** Eh? Oh . . . I see, you think this is furniture polish. Ridiculous, what would furniture polish be doing in a wine bottle? No, no, discovered our mistake soon as you left . . .
**Sara** Oh, good, we were so worried we'd ruin Celia's dinner party.
**Jeremy** No fear of that so long as we keep to a tight schedule. Cheers. (*He runs to the kitchen door*)
**Sara** Jeremy. Is something wrong?
**Jeremy** Wrong? What could be wrong? No, just Celia . . . a bit nervous you know . . . newly-wed and all that . . . we're preparing to have it, out on the patio . . . (*He moves to exit—then pauses, and confidentially*) It'll be the first time we've had it out there.

*Jeremy exits into the kitchen*

*Sara and Humphrey stare at each other*

**Sara** On the patio!
**Humphrey** Well, it *is* a rather pleasant evening.
**Sara** (*bemused*) But on the patio? (*Sudden thought*) It must be very uncomfortable, surely?

*Celia enters from the kitchen, and begins to pick up four scatter cushions from around the room. As she moves to exit:*

**Celia** You must think we're being awfully rude?

**Humphrey** Oh, no, not at all . . .

*Celia exits into the kitchen*

But I can't speak for the neighbours.

*Sara starts to lay up the table as requested*

**Sara** Better give me a hand.
**Humphrey** (*starting to lay up too*) Oh, I don't think there's any great rush.

*Jeremy enters from the kitchen rubbing his hands*

**Jeremy** Right, that's that then. (*At Sara*) Now how about you?
**Sara** What!?
**Jeremy** A sherry or something before dinner . . .?
**Celia** (*off*) Jeremy, I need you again.
**Jeremy** Excuse me.

*Jeremy exits into the kitchen again*

*A long pause – then:*

**Humphrey** I know you can take courses in speed *reading*.

*They continue laying up the table*

**Sara** I suppose it's our fault really.
**Humphrey** Eh?!
**Sara** Well, no doubt they expected to come back and be alone . . . just the two of them . . . and . . . well, you know.
**Humphrey** Only too well—I had the same expectations.
**Sara** Yes, but it is their honeymoon. My honeymoon wasn't like that.
**Humphrey** Nor mine.
**Sara** I had a beautiful time.
**Humphrey** Smashing.
**Sara** Romantic . . .
**Humphrey** Definitely.
**Sara** And passionate. Yes, I remember now . . . Peregrine did used to be passionate.
**Humphrey** Thelma was a raver. An absolute raver.
**Sara** I wonder why he changed. Or when? Or was it me?

*Celia enters from the kitchen, carrying a tray of soup, which she puts down*

**Celia** Ah . . . now you sit there . . . you there . . . (*She lays out four bowls of soup and begins to eat very fast, with constant glances over her shoulder to the kitchen door*)

*Humphrey and Sara stare at her*

**Humphrey** Shouldn't we wait for Jeremy?
**Celia** Oh, he's on the second course.
**Sara** What?

**Celia** Preparing it. He insisted that we go ahead ... and he'll be in any moment ...

*Jeremy enters from the kitchen, eating. He replaces the salt shaker, and takes the pepper mill—and, around his mouthful of food:*

**Jeremy** *Bon appétit.*

*Jeremy exits into the kitchen again*

**Celia** You see, I told you he'd be in.

*They eat, baffled—Celia at a fast rate*

**Sara** (*at last—tentatively*) We never did ask you about your honeymoon.
**Humphrey** Yes, back a week early ... what was it—the weather turn sour on you?
**Celia** It was one thing after another ... the hotel, the food ... and the final straw was Jeremy on top of the wardrobe ...
**Humphrey** Eh?
**Celia** I'd better see what's keeping him.

*She gathers up her now empty plate and exits into the kitchen*

**Sara** On top of the wardrobe?
**Humphrey** It makes the patio sound positively luxurious!

*Jeremy enters, rubbing his hands together*

**Jeremy** Ah. How are we doing, eh? (*He sits down and starts to eat very fast*)

*A moment—then:*

**Humphrey** Celia was telling us about your honeymoon.
**Jeremy** Oh, yes ... suppose she mentioned the famous wardrobe incident?
**Humphrey** Well, yes, as a matter of fact ...
**Jeremy** It would have been all right if Celia hadn't screamed. I suppose it was the shock. She'd never seen one as big as that before, you see. But she coped magnificently. Took her slipper to it!

*Humphrey chokes, starts to cough*

**Sara** I think some water ...
**Jeremy** Water ... ? Yes, water ... (*He hurries to the kitchen—and then*) By the way—Celia thinks the patio is such a success that she wants to have it out there as often as possible. Weather permitting.

*This causes Sara to cough and choke. Jeremy raises a finger of each hand*

TWO glasses of water.

*Jeremy exits into the kitchen*

*Humphrey and Sara stare at each other as they cough in unison*

*Celia enters from the kitchen, carrying two glasses of water*

**Celia** Oh dear, I hope it wasn't too much pepper?

*Humphrey and Sara take the glasses. Humphrey sips, and in a hoarse voice:*

**Humphrey** No . . . Jeremy told us about what's going on out on the patio.
**Celia** Oh, good, he's explained has he? Mind you, I agree with him—after all, there are so very few weeks in the year when one *can* do it outside . . . it seems such a pity to waste such an opportunity.
**Sara** (*recovered at last*) Opportunity?
**Celia** I suppose in a hot climate—like Africa—they have it outside all the time . . .
**Humphrey** (*shaken*) Well, yes . . . I suppose they——
**Celia** (*interjection*) Except during the Monsoon of course. Or is that India . . . ? Anyway, we can only do it every once in a while . . . and it's so fortunate that you are here to join in . . .
**Sara** What?!

*Jeremy enters from the kitchen*

**Jeremy** I suppose everybody here wants stuffing?!

*Sara and Humphrey choke and cough again—and, as one, reach for the water glasses*

**Celia** Oh, Jeremy . . . I've just been telling them that we intend having the main course outside on the patio.
**Humphrey** (*recovering*) The main course?!
**Sara** (*recovering*) Oh, you mean . . .? (*At Humphrey*) What they meant was . . .
**Celia** How are things outside?
**Jeremy** *About two minutes away from being finished* (*At Celia*) So you'll be able to start serving very soon now . . .

*Celia gets up from the table, Jeremy moves to sit down*

Oh, but I feel I've been neglecting you.

*Celia now clears away the soup things*

Put it down to over-zealousness. I did so want the patio to be . . . "right" . . . empty. With not another person in sight. And . . . (*at Celia*) . . . within two minutes . . . give or take a second or three . . . it *will be empty* . . . and, had there been any other persons there, they would be moving on.
**Humphrey** (*even more baffled*) I . . . I would like to propose a toast. (*He stands up, glass in hand*) You have been a brick, Jeremy—this evening might easily have been a disastrous event . . . but, no. On the contrary . . . so far it has been . . . somewhat unconventional . . . but then, the present circumstances *are* unconventional . . . but you have coped, Jeremy. You and Celia. And so I raise my glass to my host——

*Celia exits*

—and hostess. (*He reacts to the closed door*)
**Jeremy** Never mind, I'll tell her.
**Sara** No, we can tell her.

*Jeremy reacts*

We *will* be seeing her again. Won't we?
**Jeremy** Naturally. You are, after all, our guests. Honoured guests. And what manner of host is it who deserts his guests?
**Celia** (*off*) Jeremy!
**Jeremy** Excuse me.

*Jeremy exits into the kitchen fast*

*Humphrey and Sara stare at each other*

*Syd enters from the cellar, carrying the (about half) length of pipe*

**Syd** I'm on top of the situation. Won't be long now.

*Syd exits through the front door*

**Sara** (*staring after Syd*) I thought that man left ages ago!
**Humphrey** Obviously he's not built in the Speedy Winthrop mould. *They* could have replumbed Buckingham Palace by now!
**Sara** Yes. (*She considers*) He is an awfully *quick* young man, isn't he?

*Jeremy enters from the kitchen*

**Jeremy** Now!
**Humphrey** Now?
**Jeremy** Yes, there's no time to lose . . . I'll bring the wine . . . you bring that . . . you take that . . .

*Jeremy loads Sara and Humphrey with condiments, glasses, etc. Then he starts to urge them towards the kitchen door*

This way . . .
**Humphrey** (*looking at Sara*) Awfully quick.

*Jeremy, Humphrey and Sara exit into the kitchen. As the door closes . . .*

*Celia enters through the french doors—checks that all is clear*

**Celia** Now!

*Peregrine and Thelma enter through the french doors*

Right. Sit yourselves down, and I'll be serving the dessert immediately.

*Celia exits into the kitchen*

*Peregrine and Thelma regard each other*

**Peregrine** I was right the first time. It *is* some kind of race. (*Quickly, brooking no argument*) And what about all this palaver about bringing us right around the house and through that door?!
**Thelma** She explained *that*.
**Peregrine** Eh?
**Thelma** She said she wanted to bring us by the pretty route.
**Peregrine** Past the dustbins!?

**Thelma** Perry! After all, this *is* their house ... and they *are* being very understanding.

**Peregrine** You're right. I see the plan now.

**Thelma** What?

**Peregrine** They understand the situation—but they're not completely accepting it.

**Thelma** What do you mean?

**Peregrine** They are trying to exhaust us. Deprive us of all energy so that, when we retire to bed ... which ... given current par for the course, would be thirty-two seconds from now ...

*Jeremy enters from the kitchen, carrying a tray with desserts on it*

Correction. Twenty-eight seconds!

**Jeremy** Ah, here we are again then ... Oh, do sit down, do sit down ... strawberries and cream ... Cream? Cream!

*Jeremy exits into the kitchen again*

*Peregrine and Thelma stare at the strawberries*

**Thelma** I don't understand you, Perry—why *would* they want to exhaust us?

**Peregrine** So that we are unable to.

**Thelma** Unable to? What?

**Peregrine** *You* know.

**Thelma** Oh, that. I'm too tired to think about it at the moment.

**Peregrine** You see! *You see!*

*Celia enters carrying cream. She sits down, starts to serve strawberries and cream*

**Celia** (*during this*) You'll both take strawberries and cream ... ? Sugar's there if you want it ...

*Jeremy enters from the kitchen—very exhausted—he mops his brow—and sits down*

*Celia mechanically serves a plate for him too*

**Thelma** Well, this *is* nice.

**Peregrine** We were beginning to wonder if it would ever happen?

**Celia**  
**Jeremy** } (*together*) Eh?

**Peregrine** The two of you seated at the table at the same time.

**Celia**  
**Jeremy** } (*together*) The two of us!? (*They stare at each other*)

**Jeremy** Oh my God!

*Jeremy exits into the kitchen fast*

*They stare after him—a beat—they would start eating—but:*

*Jeremy enters from the kitchen to grab up the salt shaker, taking the sugar shaker by mistake*

The salt never seems to be where it ought to be!

*Jeremy exits into the kitchen with the shaker*

*Celia smiles sweetly at her astonished guests*

**Celia** I do hope you're enjoying dinner?
**Thelma** Well, it *is* different ...
**Peregrine** To say the least ... (*He has a shaker in his hand*) Oh, this appears to be salt.
**Celia** What!? (*She snatches the shaker from him and rushes to the kitchen— as she gets to the door ...*)

*It opens and Jeremy enters carrying HIS shaker*

Salt!
**Jeremy** Sugar!

*Celia exits into the kitchen with HER shaker*

*Jeremy comes to put HIS shaker on the table*

My goodness, that was a near thing. Imagine—potatoes covered in sugar.
**Thelma** But we're eating strawberries, Jeremy.
**Jeremy** Of course you are. (*He sits down and starts to eat very fast*) I hope Celia's been entertaining you?
**Thelma** Spasmodically.
**Peregrine** I say, old chap ... has Celia ever been an athlete of any kind ... hundred yards dash, that kind of thing?
**Jeremy** No, I don't think so.
**Peregrine** It's probably nerves then.
**Jeremy** (*pushing his plate away*) Mmm ... delicious. Excuse me.

*Jeremy exits into the kitchen*

**Thelma** Perry ... ?
**Peregrine** Yes, darling.
**Thelma** Do you think they'll be moving us on somewhere again?
**Peregrine** Well, we *are* on the last course. I think that, if we decline the cheese and biscuits they might take pity on us and allow us to rest in one place for a while.
**Thelma** It was such an unusual reason for bringing us in from the patio.
**Peregrine** Well, we don't know for certain that there *isn't* a killer swan on the prowl!
**Thelma** (*hesitantly*) Perry ... you don't think Winthrop might be the teeniest bit unhinged?
**Peregrine** Oh, no ... nervous, I grant you that ... but as you've already pointed out ... they are newly-weds! No, no, Jeremy is a perfectly rational young man——

*Jeremy enters from the kitchen in a panic*

**Jeremy** (*shrieking*) Outside ... quick ... everybody outside!

*His panic is contagious and without waiting for explanations, Peregrine and Thelma allow Jeremy to hustle them out through the french doors*

*A pause—then Humphrey enters from the kitchen—goes straight up the stairs and into the bathroom! The door closes*

*Celia enter from the kitchen, looking at her watch, then at the bathroom door*

*The kitchen door opens and Sara enters*

**Sara** Celia, my dear, can I give you a hand with . . .? (*She stops as she sees the table laid up for dessert*) Oh, yes I can . . . I'll clear away the soup things for you . . . (*She starts to stack the strawberry bowls, which are identical china to the earlier soup bowls*)
**Celia** Oh, no . . . really . . .
**Sara** Oh, but I insist.
**Celia** No, no, *I* insist . . .
**Sara** We'll compromise and do it together, shall we?
**Celia** Very well, but please hurry.

*Celia starts to gather up plates, etc., Sara helping*

**Sara** How extraordinary!
**Celia** What? What!?
**Sara** At the bottom of this soup plate—it looks awfully like a strawberry!
**Celia** My secret ingredient. It gives the vichyssoise that extra taste of summer, don't you think? Right, are we ready then?
**Sara** Yes. Now, into the kitchen with these . . .

*Celia looks beyond Sara to where . . .*

*Jeremy enters at the french doors—asking in mime if all is clear yet*

**Celia** (*to Jeremy*) Not yet!

*Sara is startled*

*Jeremy exits*

(*To Sara*) Now . . . now . . . hurry!

*Celia hustles a startled Sara—both carrying plates, etc., into the kitchen*

*A pause—then the bathroom door opens—Humphrey enters and descends the stairs*

*Jeremy enters through the french doors, sees Humphrey*

**Jeremy** (*a shriek of anguish*) Ah!

*Humphrey spins round*

Ah . . . there you are . . . wondered where you'd been.
**Humphrey** You know where I've been!
**Jeremy** Quite so. Quite so . . . and we're all waiting out on the patio for you to tell us all about it . . .

*Jeremy in utter panic, with constant looks back towards the french doors—hustles Humphrey forward—they exit into the kitchen*

*Peregrine and Thelma enter*

**Peregrine** It's a high price to pay for our infidelity!
**Thelma** Eh?
**Peregrine** I have to enter into partnership with a lunatic. A *retarded* lunatic!
**Thelma** I agree it *was* strange.
**Peregrine** Strange!? Rushing us out into the garden to see how pretty the house looks at night!
**Thelma** Well, Perry . . . with the lights and everything, it did look rather cosy!
**Peregrine** You are missing the point, Thelma . . . he hustled us out there heedless of our safety—with a killer swan on the prowl! My God, I need a brandy now. (*He starts to pour a brandy*)
**Thelma** Don't you think we should wait for our host and hostess?
**Peregrine** Together—or separately? Don't bother, as they dash by I'll wave!

*Jeremy enters from the kitchen carrying a tray of coffee cups—he puts it down on the table*

**Jeremy** With you in a moment . . .

*He half waves, exits into the kitchen*

*Peregrine fully waves back—then catches himself at it—and reacts*

**Thelma** (*weakly*) I think I'll join you.

*Peregrine pours Thelma a brandy too*

We should drink to something.
**Peregrine** (*venomously*) What about "absent friends"?!

*Syd enters through the front door—the pipe again cut by about half now*

**Syd** Soon get to the bottom of it now.
**Peregrine** Eh?
**Syd** The situation I'm on top of it. Soon get to the bottom of it. (*Confidently, indicating the pipe*) I've been measuring it from the wrong end.

*Syd exits into the cellar*

**Peregrine** Do you think insanity can be contagious?

*Celia enters from the kitchen, carrying a coffee pot and creamer. As she starts to pour:*

**Celia** Cream with your strawberries?

*They stare at her*

I mean with your coffee! You must forgive me, I feel rather confused this evening. You'll sugar your own, won't you?

*Celia exits*

*A pause*

**Peregrine** One thing utterly baffles me.
**Thelma** What's that?
**Peregrine** How the Winthrops ever actually *met*.
**Thelma** I think they met on a ship ...
**Peregrine** Two ships! It would have had to have been *two* ships. Passing each other in the night ... at about ninety miles an hour!

*Jeremy enters from the kitchen*

**Jeremy** Gosh, you're drinking alone. Can't allow that. (*He pours a brandy*) Cheers ...

*He downs it and exits into the kitchen ... while Thelma and Peregrine still have their glasses only just lifted to their lips. They stare after him—then:*

**Peregrine** I never realized before how clever those Tour de France cyclists are. Eating and drinking on the move ... (*He discreetly presses his abdomen*) I'm not sure my digestive system will ever be the same again. I think it would be unwise to retire to bed on the verge of nervous breakdown. I really do feel the need for a stroll ... at a snail's pace ... no, not quite as fast as that.
**Thelma** I think that's a good idea ... but it's turning chilly, we'll need our coats ...

*Thelma and Peregrine ascend to the bedroom. Even as they exit into the bedroom ...*

*Celia enters from the kitchen and sees them exit*

*Jeremy enters from the kitchen—stretching and yawning elaborately so as to make Peregrine and Thelma tired—as he does so, he turns this way and that, looking for them*

**Jeremy** Gosh, I'm tired ... I will be thinking of turning in soon ... you must be tired too ... Where are they?!
**Celia** Gone to their room. (*Celia sits down heavily*)
**Jeremy** Thank God.

*Jeremy sits down beside her. They start to relax a bit. A pause*

They didn't say good-night. I say, you don't think we upset them in any way, do you?
**Celia** I don't see how we can have. After all, we've hardly seen them all evening.
**Jeremy** Yes.
**Celia** They *might* have said good-night—when I sprinted in with the cream.
**Jeremy** You don't think we rushed them too much, do you?
**Celia** No. (*Then she adds*) Mind you, I was never here long enough to find out.
**Jeremy** Yes.

*A pause—then:*

**Celia** I'm numb at the moment.

**Jeremy** Yes, was getting a bit cold out there.

**Celia** I wonder when it will hit me.

**Jeremy** Eh?

**Celia** Later, I expect. I'm still in shock at the moment, but when it——

**Jeremy** (*interjecting*) Shock?

**Celia** At what we've done.

**Jeremy** We've done damned well. I'm proud of you, darling ... you coped magnificently. A marvellous dinner.

**Celia** Which one? The Jessel and Ward one ... or the Ward and Jessel ...?
(*Even as she says it—she realizes and turns to stare at the kitchen door*)
Jeremy. There are two still out there!

*Jeremy turns to the kitchen door*

*It opens—Humphrey and Sara enter*

**Jeremy** Ah, I was just coming to fetch you. (*He goes through the elaborate yawning bit again*) My gosh, the night air is tiring, isn't it ...? Bed soon ... but you'll have a brandy first?

**Humphrey** Hope you don't mind, we thought we'd skip the brandy and go straight to bed. Sara is feeling a ... er ... little dazed ...

**Jeremy** Oh, I am sorry—is there anything we can do?

**Sara** Oh, no you've done enough already. More than enough. You must be exhausted ...

**Humphrey** I know we are!

**Sara** Thank you for a most ... interesting meal, Celia ... Jeremy. Goodnight.

*Ad-lib "Good-nights". Humphrey and Sara ascend to exit into their bedroom*

*As soon as the door closes—Jeremy and Celia wilt*

**Celia** It's over. Thank God, it's all over.

**Jeremy** Not quite, darling.

*She looks at him*

There's still the morning. Breakfast.

**Celia** It's coming.

**Jeremy** Eh?

**Celia** I can feel it coming. The hysteria.

**Jeremy** No, darling ...

**Celia** I can't help it.

**Jeremy** Then try and scream in a whisper.

**Celia** The thought of the morning. Breakfast. Eggs perambulating from one room to the next ...

**Jeremy** Don't worry, darling. I'll think of something.

*Celia stares at him*

What's the matter? Have you lost confidence in me!?

**Celia** Jeremy, my confidence in you suffered a severe set-back when you invented the killer swan.

**Jeremy** What? I thought that was rather a clever touch.

**Celia** It was complete nonsense. Everyone knows swans don't fly at night.

**Jeremy** Hmm. You're right. It should have been a killer owl.

**Celia** *Jeremy* ... ! *Tomorrow morning!*

**Jeremy** Don't panic. Please don't panic ... it's contagious. We will think of something.

**Celia** (*regarding him*) I suppose we *could* give them both breakfast in bed ...?

**Jeremy** You see ... it's not impossible ... Now come on ... while we put our minds to it ... let's get these things cleared away ...

*Celia and Jeremy gather up dishes. They exit into the kitchen*

*A pause—then Thelma and Peregrine enter from the bedroom, wearing coats now. They descend the stairs*

**Peregrine** I think I should point out, Thelma, that *Sara* has always been very sympathetic on occasions like this.

**Thelma** But dyspepsia is so unromantic.

**Peregrine** Sympathetic. And, I now realize—incredibly tolerant.

**Thelma** I think *I* should point out, Peregrine, that had Humphrey accompanied me on this weekend ... his intentions *would* have been more predictable. But more fun.

*Thelma and Peregrine exit through the french doors*

*Jeremy and Celia enter from the kitchen to gather up more dishes*

**Celia** Yes, that might be a solution.

*They start to gather up dishes—then Celia pauses thoughtfully*

But if the house burns down, won't they find *four* charred bodies amongst the ruins?

**Jeremy** Well, it was just a thought.

*Celia and Jeremy exit into the kitchen*

*Sara enters from the bedroom—clutching her coat around her. A beat later Humphrey enters from the bedroom, holding his coat and pursuing her as she descends the stairs*

**Humphrey** Darling, I still think I can calm you down in my own inimitable way—up there ...

**Sara** You were rushing me, Humphrey ... and I've been rushed enough already this evening. I need some air ...

**Humphrey** All right, all right, we'll stroll ... but not too far, eh? Then straight back to bed ...

*They are at the french doors when he grabs and embraces her*

Oh, Sara ... Oh Sara ... Oh my God!

*This as he gazes off through the french doors. Sara follows his gaze*

**Sara**  Peregrine!
**Humphrey**  And Thelma!

*They retreat from the french doors*

**Sara**  But how ... *how!*
**Humphrey**  They obviously both got home earlier than expected ... phoned me in Munich ...
**Sara**  Me in Bristol ...
**Humphrey**  Found out neither of us were there.
**Sara**  And concluded we'd come here ... Humphrey—what are we going to do?
**Humphrey**  The same as them. Quick ...

*He runs up the stairs—exits into the bedroom—comes out carrying two suitcases—then starts to hustle Sara out of the front door. As it closes ...*

*Celia enters from the kitchen, gathers up dishes. She pauses to gaze up the stairs*

*Jeremy enters from kitchen*

**Celia**  I still can't believe it.
**Jeremy**  Believe what, darling ... ?
**Celia**  That they are all four of them up there ... safely tucked up in bed ...
**Jeremy**  (*preening himself*) When it comes to arranging things I'm no fool you know, darling.

*Carrying the last of the dishes, Jeremy and Celia exit into the kitchen*

*Thelma and Peregrine enter through the french doors in a terrific panic. They hurry across the area and up the stairs*

**Thelma**  But how, Perry, *how!?*
**Peregrine**  Does it matter how? They're here—your husband, and my wife!
**Thelma**  They obviously got back early ... then phoned me in Exeter ...
**Peregrine**  Me in Paris ... then concluded we'd both come here.
**Thelma**  What are we going to do?!
**Peregrine**  The same as them.

*He collects their cases from the bedroom then hustles Thelma out to exit through the french doors*

*Syd enters from the cellar, wiping his hands on a rag, an air of angry resignation about him*

**Syd**  Bleeding Albanians! (*He picks up the phone, dials a number. On the phone*) Charley? Syd again. ... No, no, it's the last time I promise. It's getting too dangerous down there. ... Yes, you surmise right, Charley. ... No, I haven't fixed it. It *was* all going well though—but I'll tell you, Charley, there ought to be a law against having a sewage pipe *that* close to the mains..... Yes, Charley, definitely a public hazard—so it's all down to you now. (*He listens*) Well, of course *I* can call the Water Board Emergency Service, but they'll only call you, won't they? This way saves everybody a lot of trouble. (*He listens*) Well, yes, everybody except you, Charley. How soon can you get your team over here? (*He listens*) No, I won't be here—missis'll be worried about me—think I've got meself into trouble or something. Also, it's brought my nerves on again. (*He listens*) No, Charley, I don't think this would be an opportune time to raise the rewiring project. Thanks—oh, and Charley—if after you've drained the cellar, you come across my tools amongst the sludge ... ? ... Charley? Charley!

*But the line is dead. Syd hangs up, shrugs—then has a swig from his flask and exits through the front door*

*A pause. Jeremy enters from the kitchen. He moves to close and lock the french doors. He goes to the sideboard, pours a small drink in a small glass—would drink—but then:*

**Jeremy**  It's my house. (*He pours the small glass into a very large glass—tops it up. Then reacts*) Yes, it *is* my house. (*Machismo rising now, a swagger coming into his step, Jeremy moves to gaze up the stairs*) And when it comes to organization, I'm no fool! You hear that, Perry ... Humph ... !? You can call me Winthrop! Are you happy in *my* bed!? Beds. Chuckling up there, are you? Well ... perhaps not *chuckling* ... but I'll bet you're very happy. Well, *I* am *not* happy. Why am I not happy ... ? Well, Perry ... Humph ... I'll tell you. *Because I am not chuckling.* In fact I have been married more than a week now, and am still chuckleless. Not even a snigger. Well ... I'm in *my* house now ... and things are going to change. (*He turns to regard the kitchen door*) You hear that, Celia? And you can call me ... sex-mad! (*He holds up a placating hand*) Yes, I know I'm a beast. *But I am also a man.* Get them off. And we'll chuckle the night away. And afterwards I'm going out to wrestle a killer swan. Or a killer owl. Depending upon what time of day it is. (*He gazes up the stairs again*) Humph? Perry? You may have my bed. Beds. But I still have my sofa. And a man's got to lay it where it lies. Kipling. Yes, a man's got to do, what a man's been thinking of doing all week. Yes. YES. Damn you all! And that includes the Morals and Clean Living Group too! (*He now moves around, turning off most of the lights until the area is seductively dim*) I'm finished with clean living ... for the time being anyway. It's chuckle time.

*Celia enters from the kitchen*

**Celia**  What are you doing?
**Jeremy**  The same as them.
**Celia**  Them?

*Jeremy points at the bedroom*

(*Realizing*) Jeremy!

**Jeremy** They've got a head start on us, but we'll catch them up. After all, I
am a lot younger. (*In a predatory manner now, he advances towards her,
stripping off his clothes*) I am going to start our long overdue, I can't-wait-
any-longer-honeymoon!
**Celia** Jeremy. No . . .
**Jeremy** Celia. Yes.
**Celia** Jeremy . . .
**Jeremy** I will not be denied. This is my house . . . and you are my wife . . .
**Celia** Jeremy . . . there's only the sofa . . .
**Jeremy** It's the sofa or nothing . . . and I'm in no mood to accept nothing.
**Celia** Surely, after this evening . . . you must be tired.
**Jeremy** On the contrary . . . my pulse is racing . . . this evening has
stimulated me . . . I suppose victory always does that to a man. And I am a
man. Celia . . . I am . . . (*He crushes her to him*)
**Celia** Oh, yes, you are, aren't you?
**Jeremy** Celia.
**Celia** Jeremy.
**Jeremy** Celia, Celia, Celia . . .

*They fall on to the couch*

**Celia** Jeremy. Jeremy . . . JEREMY!

*He starts to undress her*

Jeremy, suppose one of them comes out and finds us!?
**Jeremy** How could any of them cast the first stone and call the kettle black?
**Celia** Jeremy. I think you're mixing your metaphors.

*They embrace*

*A pause, then we hear the key go into the lock—and the front door opens—
Thelma, Humphrey, Peregrine and Sara enter, carrying their suitcases.
Lights are switched on. They all seem to be talking at once*

**Humphrey** What a coincidence . . .
**Peregrine** Four minds with but a single thought.
**Sara** You must have been just as surprised to see us . . .
**Thelma** As we were to see you.
**Humphrey** Soon as I arrived back . . .
**Peregrine** Earlier than expected . . .
**Sara** I tried to call you . . .
**Thelma** When you were not there . . . I naturally concluded . . .
**Humphrey** That you'd decided to take the Winthrops up on their offer . . .
**Thelma** Then I bumped into Peregrine . . .
**Humphrey** I bumped into Sara . . .
**All** And here we are . . . all turning up on the same doorstep . . . at the same
time . . . What a happy coincidence!

*During this, of course—Jeremy and Celia have reacted—not only to them—
but eventually to the fact that THEY are partially undressed. Also during
this—Sara, Thelma, Peregrine and Humphrey—each separately sees and*

*acknowledges Jeremy's presence crouched on the sofa—then immediately ignores him. Jeremy remains pressed flat—with Celia almost under him as Thelma, Peregrine, Humphrey and Sara start to ascend the stairs. Then Humphrey pauses—looks right back at Jeremy*

**Humphrey** I say, wouldn't it be fortuitous if the Winthrops came home unexpectedly early too? *Like tomorrow morning.*

*Peregrine pauses, turns to look at Jeremy*

**Peregrine** Very fortuitous. Because I want to speak to him about the vacant partnership. *I'm sure, if he plays his cards right, he'll get it.*

*Sara turns—and at Jeremy*

**Sara** *Oh, I'm definitely sure he will.*

*Thelma turns, and at Jeremy*

**Thelma** *I'd stake my reputation on it.*

*At the top of the stairs now, they pause*

**All** Well, good-night . . . see you in the morning.

> *Thelma and Peregrine enter the room they have been occupying. Sara and Humphrey enter the room they have been occupying. The doors close—a pause—then suddenly both doors open again—and Thelma and Peregrine and Sara and Humphrey change rooms*
>
> How silly of us . . . !
>
> *The doors close. A pause. Suddenly both doors open—Sara and Thelma change rooms—each carrying and swinging stockings and suspenders. A look is exchanged—then each enters the room to join her proper/respective husband at last. The doors close—with an air of finality*

*Jeremy, who has been crouched throughout all this, finally stands up and looks at the bedrooms—stunned. In getting up, he has finally released Celia from beneath him. She excitedly sits up*

**Celia** Oh, Jeremy. The partnership. You're going to get it, Jeremy. You're going to get it!

*Jeremy slowly turns to gaze at her*

**Jeremy** Too bloody right I am!

*As Jeremy starts to grab at Celia—off-stage we hear the sound of several vehicles arriving—lights hit an outside window—and then there is a hammering at the door. Jeremy and Celia are astonished*

**Male Voice** (*off*) Water Board Emergency!

CURTAIN

# FURNITURE AND PROPERTY LIST

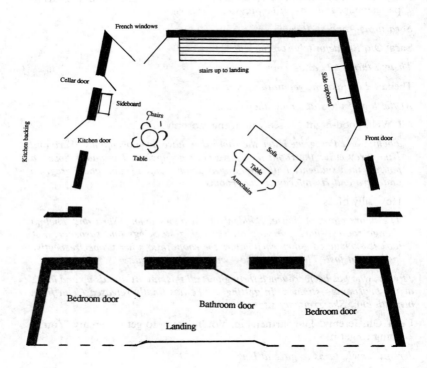

## ACT I

*On stage:* Dining table
4 chairs
Sideboard. *In it:* plates. *On it:* bottles of drink, glasses, telephone, table
  lamp. *In drawer:* napkins, cutlery
Sofa. *On it:* scatter cushions
2 armchairs
Coffee table. *On it:* ashtray, box of cigarettes
Side table. *On it:* lamp

Key outside front door (on hook or under mat)
Key in french doors
Mirror on wall upstairs

*Off stage:* 2 suitcases **(Jeremy)**
2 small cases, bottle of champagne, box of chocolates, package containing
    stockings and suspenders **(Humphrey)**
Package containing stockings and suspenders **(Humphrey)**
2 small cases **(Peregrine)**
Key **(Peregrine)**
Strange piece of piping **(Syd)**
Bags of groceries **(Jeremy** and **Celia)**
Very long piece of pipe **(Syd)**
Unlit cigarette **(Sara)**

*Personal:* **Syd:** flask of drink *(required throughout)*
**Sara:** lighter in robe pocket
**Celia:** wrist-watch *(required throughout)*
**Jeremy:** wrist-watch *(required throughout)*


## ACT II

*Set:*        Dining table partially laid for four

*Off stage:* Piece of pipe **(Syd)**
Toolbag **(Syd)**
More things for the table **(Celia)**
Large pipe wrench **(Syd)**
Bowl of *petits fours* **(Celia)**
Uncorked bottle of wine **(Jeremy)**
More things for the table **(Celia)**
Length of pipe **(Syd)**
Bowl of croûtons **(Celia)**
Tray with 4 bowls of soup **(Celia)**
Tray with 4 bowls of soup **(Jeremy)**
Cutlery, condiments **(Jeremy)**
Bottle of wine, glasses **(Jeremy)**
Tray with 4 bowls of soup **(Celia)**
Salt shaker, mouthful of food **(Jeremy)**
2 glasses of water **(Celia)**
$\frac{1}{2}$ length of pipe **(Syd)**
Tray with 4 bowls of strawberries, sugar shaker **(Celia)**
Jug of cream **(Celia)**
Sugar shaker **(Jeremy)**
Tray with coffee cups **(Jeremy)**
Shorter length of pipe **(Syd)**
Coffee pot, jug of cream **(Celia)**
Coat **(Humphrey)**
2 suitcases **(Humphrey)**
2 suitcases **(Peregrine)**
Rag **(Syd)**
Suitcases **(Thelma, Humphrey, Peregrine, Sara)**
Stockings, suspenders **(Sara)**
Stockings, suspenders **(Thelma)**

# LIGHTING PLOT

Practical fittings required: wall-brackets, table lamps, landing light

Interior. A country cottage. The same scene throughout

ACT I   Afternoon

*To open*   General interior lighting; balmy summer lighting outside

*No cues*

ACT II   Evening

*To open:*   Wall-brackets, table lamps, landing light on; dusk outside.
*Becoming progressively darker during Act*

*Cue* 1    As **Jeremy** turns off lights                                    (Page 51)
          *Snap off lights as he does*

*Cue* 2    As **Thelma, Humphrey, Peregrine** and **Sara** enter and switch on   (Page 52)
          lights
          *Snap up lights as they do*

*Cue* 3    As **Jeremy** starts to grab at **Celia**                          (Page 53)
          *Vehicle headlights hit window*

# EFFECTS PLOT

## ACT I

*Cue* 1   Shortly after CURTAIN rises                                              (Page 1)
*Taxi drives up, stops, doors open and close, taxi drives away*

*Cue* 2   **Celia** exits into kitchen; **Jeremy** haplessly follows her            (Page 3)
*Taxi drives up, stops, doors open and close*

*Cue* 3   As **Sara** enters cottage                                               (Page 3)
*Taxi drives away*

## ACT II

*Cue* 4   As **Jeremy** starts to grab at **Celia**                                (Page 53)
*Sound of several vehicles arriving and stopping, doors opening
    and closing*